Modernizing Indian Defence

Attention Authors

Manas Publications is fighting a war to tell the world that India can win the battle not only by the bullet but also by pen. We are converting fighters into writers. There is no dearth of intellectuals in our country, however, their knowledge is confined to them only. No sincere effort has been made by any other publisher to channelise their knowledge, which is why the talent of every intellectual remains latent. An author always presents the raw material in the shape of a manuscript and it is the job of the publisher to convert it to a finished product. Manas has been continually motivating intellectuals and publishing their manuscripts for more than two decades and would like to publish your manuscript too. If you or your colleagues have a manuscript ready for publication or are working on it, contact us with a detailed synopsis and list of contents. Manas can also suggest you a suitable title for writing related to your area of expertise. Manas is known for its publishing quality. We take utmost care in publishing and also give wide publicity to the book and its author through our national and international distribution network.

Modernizing Indian Defence

Lt Gen PC Katoch
UYSM, AVSM, SC

Air Marshal SR Deshpande
PVSM, AVSM, VM (G)

Manas Publications
(We Convert Fighters into Writers)
New Delhi-110002 (INDIA)

Manas Publications
(Publishers, Library Suppliers, Importers & Exporters)
4402/5-A, Ansari Road (Opp. HDFC Bank)
Darya Ganj, New Delhi-110 002 (India)
Off. & 23260783, 23265523, Res. & 23842660
Fax: 011-23272766
E-mail: manaspublications@vsnl.com
manaspublications@yahoo.com

ISBN 978-81-7049-316-7
₹ 595/-

Typeset at
Manas Publications

Printed in India at
RK Print Services, Delhi
and published by Mrs Suman Lata for
Manas Publications, 4402/5-A, Ansari Road
(Opp. HDFC Bank),
Darya Ganj, New Delhi-110 002 (INDIA)

Contents

Preface

The Indian defence forces have, over the last six decades and more, played their parts in not only fulfilling their primary mandate of preserving the nation's borders but have helped India emerge as a confident and a responsible nation state by its commitment to uphold the core values of the Indian society.

India faces multifarious threats and challenges, border management and maritime security. India has disputes over land borders with China and Pakistan. There are other tensions in India's neighbourhood. Ongoings in Afghanistan need no recounting. Political infighting is keeping Nepal mired in conflicts within. Sanctuaries and training camps of some of the insurgent groups in restive southern Bhutan are a cause of concern. So is the case along the Indo-Myanmar border where the writ of the military junta in Yangon does not run. Bangladesh's commitment to curb anti-India activities apart, the issues of border management and illegal migration remain. Tamil agitations in Sri Lanka cause ripples in India. Aggressive Chinese efforts to increase its presence in these countries add to India's security concerns.

India must also take note of the unfolding power play of global interests in the Indian Ocean region. Protection of air spaces over these land and maritime frontier, as over our island territories, denotes the operational challenge of air force. At present, country is also facing three challenges to internal security: terrorism, insurgency in north eastern states, and Left Wing extremism or Naxalism. Armed forces, essentially the army will have to attend to such threats within. Then there are also natural disasters to attend to.

In the overall context of the foregoing discussion, the security challenge facing India is diverse, complex and evolving. Prime Minister Manmohan Singh has observed "To meet national security challenge, our strategy has to be based on three broad pillars. First is to strengthen ourselves economically and technologically; second, to acquire adequate defence capability to counter and rebut threats to our security, and the third, to seek partnerships both on the strategic front and on the economic and technological front to widen our policy and development options".

Defence modernization is a priority for the armed forces. The government carried out defence reforms in 2001 to evolve integrated and joint structures for higher defence organization in order to face the emerging threats and consequently achieve the desired levels of modernization. At the present juncture, our defence forces are in transition from industrial age forces to knowledge age forces with a portion being equipped with state-of-the-art weapons. While the army has larger element of industrial age forces, the navy and the air force, which are more technology intensive forces and less manpowered intensive, are much better on the equipment profile since future wars will see limits of high technology warfare. The contributors being expert in their field with vast experience have highlighted each aspect of modernization in order to make the book a guiding tool for the defence authorities who should always bear in mind that wars, now, are not won by machines but by men behind the machines.

Chapter 1

Indian Army: Changing Nature of Conflict

General Deepak Kapoor,
*PVSM, AVSM, SM, VSM (Retd)**

The character of warfare is shaped and determined more by the political, social, economic and strategic imbalance, than it is by changes that occur in military science. The break-up of Soviet Union in 1991 led to the end of the Cold War. The period that followed came to an abrupt end on 11 September 2001. The world has never been the same again as new forms of conflict emerged on the horizon, which created a situation of "no war-no peace". If we look back in history, it took almost 100 years to evolve from 1st to 2nd generation warfare, but it took just about 25 years to shift from 2nd to 3rd generation warfare between WW-I and WW-II. But the 4th and 5th generation warfare is evolving near simultaneously. There is a paradigm

*The writer was Chief of the Army Staff, Indian Army.

shift in the nature of future wars and conflict. Understanding the consequences of such engagement is vital because it determines the concept and doctrines for the future.

The period between 1945 and 1991 saw the evolution of 3rd generation war, mainly conflict between states in a situation of "no war-no peace". This period was marked by the Cold War era as well. But at the same time, another way of waging war was evolving. The use of violence to impose ideology, struggles for self-determination and wars against political, economical and social suppression became the trend. This was the period when non-state actors started to emerge as future adversaries. Some of these non-state actors also emerged as tools for proxy war on behalf of one nation against another.

Armed conflicts have cross border linkages and are shifting from rural insurgencies to urban terrorism. In some countries, conflict has reached almost every household and is no more restricted to the borders or traditional war zones. Land boundaries and the neighbourhood are no longer of much relevance in the changing nature of conflict. There is still uncertainty about the way the 21st century will shape out, but one thing we know for sure is that it is a period which will see constant turmoil - a period of neither war nor peace.

Another disturbing trend which has surfaced is that well armed groups and individuals with the potential to support, or trigger sub-conventional military operations are rapidly gaining strength. In the realm of "Sub-conventional" terrorism, *New York Times* columnist Thomas Friedman has referred to the phenomenon of the "super-empowered individual". The individual has been empowered in an unprecedented way to do things he could never do before. Someone can sit on an island in South East Asia and, with a computer, can access the world's knowledge, conduct international commercial transactions, or issue orders. In previous times, countries fought countries. Now groups fight countries, individuals fight countries; it is a different type of game altogether. Not only that, at times these groups could split and splinter into many sub groups, each more lethal than the other. Reigning in one may lead to the birth of another.

Therefore, it will be correct to assume that future conflicts will see these groups playing a more dominant role and state of such conflicts is likely to be more lethal and devastating. Survival of such groups will depend upon their ability to remain fluid, fast and non-linear.

Can we call this new way of war-fighting – a war on drugs, or war on radical groups or war for control of resources, or war on religious extremism? We really do not know. The battlefields are merging. Going after the poppy cultivator and heroin smuggler may go concurrently with a war on militant fundamentalist groups, in an era when drug money finds its way into terrorist wars. Sometimes, a motley group of non-state actors could make common cause against the state, all pursuing their individual agendas. In one setting they may be enemy but in another setting they may form a common front as well. A classic example is the case of Afghanistan and the NWFP-FATA region.

The war of today is not only between two states having symmetry or parity. Suicide bombings could kill as much as a conventional conflict, as the two have become entwined. Chris Donnelly says, "In the future paradigm, war may not be fought principally with weapons that kill... but economic weapons can kill even more people more efficiently, just as disease can. The war of the future could be played out with energy resources being used as a weapon, with trade being used as a weapon, with aid being used as a weapon... it is a change from thinking in terms of Defence to thinking in terms of security".

In recent years, the world has witnessed few conventional wars, though the possibility of limited war under a nuclear overhang is still very much a reality at least in the Indian sub-continent. Along with West Asia, South Asia has gradually emerged as one of the epicentres of conflict and instability. Territorial disputes, provocation by proxy wars, religious fundamentalism, radical extremism, ethnic tensions and socio-economic disparities are the hallmark of South Asia. The situation will further worsen since there is neither any political or diplomatic unity nor common ground to build a consensus to fight this new war. One country's enemy is another's friend, and as a result, conflict is assuming dangerous proportions. Nations may be forced to undertake interventions such as:-

(a) Purely on humanitarian grounds if the Diaspora of the country is under extreme threat.

(b) Sovereignty of a nation being questioned such as attacks on missions abroad and national assets.

(c) Foreign soil being used constantly for attack by state and non-state actors.

It is difficult to draw a line between wars of interest and wars of conscience; between wars of choice and wars of necessity.

Conventional wars are now not restricted to land, sea and air but two more dimensions have been added – space and cyberspace. Wars can be unleashed from drawing rooms and their impact can be as lethal as in actual combat. Therefore, they very concept of national security needs to be re-examined. It raises the question whether nations should just protect their own shores or should they go to any extent to protect their vital national interests? There is definitely a need to evolve concepts and doctrine to protect the nation's interests within and beyond the national boundaries as well.

Where does it lead us? To a future of peace and prosperity, or to a conflict-ridden future full of uncertainty? Who is the enemy and who is the threatened? Well, nations are under attack and humanity in general is threatened. Options are limited: split to suffer or unite to survive. Collective responsibility and sharing of information on the part of the nations will be key to stemming the threat from non-state actors as well as avoiding escalation of conflict between nations. Thus, cooperative security is the way to maintain peace and stability. Towards this end, capability and capacity building is imperative. The other important aspect is the capability of a nation to deter, dissuade and contain the adversaries. Escalation control and conflict termination on favourable terms is an essential part of military strategy. But conflict resolution and transformation strategies have also emerged as tools to deal with the new asymmetric and unrestricted war.

Cooperative security or multilateral military coalitions to deal with a common threat, preferably under UN aegis, will be an inescapable requirement in future. However, such an arrangement would require consensus and common platform. Joint operations off the Gulf of Aden against Somali pirates to protection of inter shipping are a case in point. However, there are still many hurdles to be overcome in order to handle common threats and challenges.

Nations will have to continue building their military capabilities, which will also necessitate shared capacity building in order to undertake joint operations. While nations have little choice but to agree to work together towards conflict resolution, the clash of interests may warrant that nations may have to fight some conflicts in isolation, for which they need to build capability and capacity. In view of the prevailing era of strategic uncertainty, the need for the armed forces to maintain readiness has become important more than ever.

(Source: Keynote address by the then COAS at the CLAWS international seminar.)

Chapter 2

Indian Army: Forever Reliable

*Lt Gen S Pattabhiraman, PVSM, AVSM, SM, VSM**

Independent India inherited a mostly British led army which having earlier helped in consolidation of the Empire was extensively battle hardened in the two World Wars. Rapid demobilisation soon after independence in 1947 was quickly and simultaneously replaced with the transformation into a committed need based army to fight the Pakistani raiders backed by its similarly transformed regular Pakistan Army.

The 1947-48 Kashmir war was followed by commitments to UN peacekeeping missions in Korea and Congo. The disastrous war with China in 1962 provided the first impetus to transform the Army into a large standing Army organized and equipped to safeguard the territorial integrity of new India.

---

*The writer is a Member of the recently formed Armed Forces Tribunal. He retired as Vice Chief of the Army Staff.

The Indian army has over the last six decades and more played its part in not only fulfilling its primary mandate of preserving the nation's borders but has helped India emerge as a confident and a responsible nation state with strong modern democratic fundamentals by its unflinching commitment to uphold the core values of the Indian society. To understand the ethos of the third largest army in the world (after China and N. Korea) it would be pertinent to view the continuing transformation in the backdrop of major landmark events having operational connotations that resulted in its present structure.

1948-Ceasefire in J&K and the 1962 Debacle

The Kashmir war of 1947-48 was thrust upon India by a cunning Pakistani leadership but soon with some outstanding acts of bravery the Indian Army turned the tide of the war and was only prevented in completing its task of liberating the whole of occupied Kashmir by the magnanimous Pandit Nehru who called a halt to operations and accepted UN intervention to resolve the dispute over the occupied portion of Kashmir. What characteristic that stood out then and what has been constant ever since the East India Company and later the British crown trained Indian Army possessed, has been the Indian soldier's steadfastness under fire and adversity, when led by competent and caring leaders.

The period between the coming into effect of the ceasefire line (CFL) and the border war with China in 1962 was unfortunately spent by the Army mostly on ceremonial duties. The Indian Army suffered its worst humiliation at the hands of the Chinese PLA, because of it being completely unprepared, having been reduced to a ceremonial army.

The war, thrust upon a poorly equipped and badly organized army with little coordination with the air force and navy (with the former sitting out the war) however proved to be a blessing in disguise and a huge wake-up call to rebuild the Army and its capacity to do its primary task of defence of the country ably. Reorganisation of major formations of the Army into self contained homogenous mountain divisions, infrastructure development and equipment upgradations as also procurement of weapons and equipment on a war footing that followed were to be mainly responsible for the brilliant success in the 1971 war.

The pacifism of the 1950s, the disastrous border war of 1962 and its aftermath are best remembered for events, occurrences and lessons that shaped the nation's future course of events and can be summarized as follows:

1) **Neighbourhood Realities:** Pakistan, due to its military ruled dictatorial polity decided to join the Western led defence pact, viz Baghdad pact, replaced by CENTO. It also seized upon the opportunity provided by India's disadvantageous border row with China to forge a permanent relationship with that country and symbolically ceded a portion of Shaksgam valley in northern occupied Kashmir to China, thus dubiously making the latter a future stakeholder in the final resolution of J&K.

2) **End of Nehru's utopian ideals:** Pandit Nehru himself was so jolted at facing the bitter truth of real politic and pragmatic self interests of nation states that he died a disheartened man. His successor the diminutive Lal Bahadur Shastri was to later lead the 1965 war effort with cold practical courage and firm resolve to lead a patriotic nation to victory at any cost.

3) **Reorganisation of the Army:** A massive effort got underway to restructure the army into all arms composed divisions, a number of them being mountain divisions and simultaneously training establishments were expanded to absorb greater numbers and the foundation for the future Indian Army of 9 lakh personnel was laid .

4) **Defence Public Sector Undertakings (PSUs):** In a renewed fillip to an already Government regulated production

of low end arms, ammunition and equipment, more PSUs were started to meet burgeoning Defence needs.

1965 War in the West

The measures taken to revamp the organizational structure and equipment profile of the Army were in the very early stages and thus did not make any impact on the Army's response to a series of Pakistan's audacious attempts between March and Sep 1965, from the Rann of Kutch to Kashmir, to test the Indian resolve to preserve its territorial integrity. A better organized higher defence structure than in 1962, ensured a unified response and resultantly the Indian Air Force saved the blushes and the Indian Navy too did its bit to decisively tilt the overall combat ratio in favour of India.

The Army in early stages of transformation, was found wanting in overall strategy, operational posturing and in war tactics but more than made up in certain individuals' personal charisma and inspirational leadership as also once again in the Indian Jawan's steadfastness and dutiful and stoic response to well led leadership. Capture of Haji Pir overlooking Pakistan's Kotli-Bhimber valley, capture of significant heights in Ladakh sector and a robust defence of the Punjab heartland which included destruction of a large number of Pakistan's main battle tanks were notable highlights of the two weeks of the final phase of the war in September in which the IAF was truly blooded in and responded magnificently in all aspects of close support.

Lal Bahadur Shastri the PM who did not hesitate in giving the go-ahead to launch the Indian counter-offensive in Punjab after setbacks in the Chamb sector in J&K, tragically died of shock at Tashkent, in Russia, where he had agreed with President Ayub Khan of Pakistan for a Soviet brokered ceasefire and pullback to positions held on the CFL, before the war, thus giving up significant areas of ground captured at great sacrifice by our troops, in Kashmir and Ladakh. The 1965 war thus ended in a stalemate. The stalemate however was to prove decisive later in 1971 when an opportunity presented itself in the restive East Bengal for the Indian Army to bring to bear the fruits of the reorganisation, and re-equipping, that commenced post the 1962 debacle (mostly with modern Soviet tanks , helicopters, artillery and engineering equipment).

1965 war thus was by itself not significant except to hasten up the reforms already underway, the most significant of these was the raising of the Border Security Force or BSF as it has come to be called. The BSF had a large complement of officers from the Army, from brigadiers down to majors and was thus instrumental in developing a military orientation to this first large Central Police Organisation (CPO) of the country. It was soon to be baptised under fire in the 1971 war under the operational control of the Army. The second most important transformation was the construction of the Ditch-cum-bund or DCB across the complete length of the Western plains from Akhnoor down to Firozpur. This in conjunction with the canal system which was being extended southwards to Rajasthan and replicated by Pakistan on its side of the Punjab plains was to usher in a doctrinal shift in the tactics of fighting a successful defensive battle along with fire power of tanks and artillery. The third most telling contribution of the war was the strategic partnership with USSR that India entered into and Russian arms and training in Russia at friendship rates that had its optimal effect in 1971 in the successful Bangladesh campaign wherein, MIG aircrafts, MI-4 and MI-8 helicopters, T-55 and PT-76 tanks, 122mm artillery pieces, trestle and floating bridges and missile boats and submarines in the Navy all contributed in the most successful military event in the history of the nation i.e. the complete and comprehensive defeat and surrender of the Pakistan army in the East.

1971 War of Liberation and its Sequel

A lot has been written about the lightning campaign in the East in Dec 1971, that ended in capture of Dacca and the surrender of the Pakistan army. Amongst military historians outside India and in foreign military circles this campaign unfortunately has not got its credit, perhaps due to the cold war mentality of not wanting to take sides in a war between two sides of the divide. The ingredients for success were indeed laid down very early in March '71 itself when Field Marshal (then Gen) FSJ Manekshaw the Army Chief, informed Mrs Indira Gandhi, the then PM that the Army needed time to train and prepare for the eventual campaign to assist the Mukti Bahini, the freedom fighters of East Pakistan. This was followed up by an unprecedented proactivity by the army's Eastern Command which set up numerous training camps to train hundreds of guerrillas of the Mukti Bahini. The Govt of West Bengal too played its part. Close coordination between the Central Govt and the West Bengal State as also between the Service HQs and the respective Command HQs of the three Services and the Intelligence agencies ensured that the Pakistan army was kept engaged and slowly sucked into border areas in penny packets. The stage was so admirably set that out of desperation Pakistan launched a pre-emptive air strike in the Western theatre thus paving the way for the Indian Army to launch a four pronged offensive towards Dacca, bypassing opposition enroute, ferrying troops in MI-4 helicopters over water obstacles, using the amphibious and deep fording capabilities of recently acquired PT-76 and T-55 tanks and carrying out a successful battalion group airborne operation at Tangail, north of Dacca. The Eastern Command of the Indian Army under Lt Gen Jagjit Singh Aurora, brought to a successful end a breathtaking campaign in 14 days, forcing the surrender of the Pakistan eastern wing of four Infantry divisions and hundreds of irregulars.

On the Western front however gains made in Ladakh and Kashmir were nullified by yet again losing ground in Chamb. But the most important legacy that has remained even after subjecting Pakistan to a crushing military defeat, is that we, as a nation, failed to capitalize on the victory for a durable peace. While the Shimla agreement that followed the aftermath of the war in the backdrop of our holding 93000 POWs successfully delineated a Line of Control in J&K to legitimize the actual positions on the ground and as a consequence brought about some period of peace between India and Pakistan until Siachen conflict in 1984, it failed to provide for any form of guarantee to keep the J&K issue strictly bilateral (though stated in the text of the agreement). In hindsight and as a result of having seen how coordination at higher levels of the government is a difficult task, it is felt that the military may not have been consulted in day to day negotiations leading to the landmark agreement. If the military had been a part of the consultation process, it would have for example suggested to wind up the United Nations Military Observer Group (UNMOGIP), who were propitiously in fact stranded on the Pakistan side of the border (having shifted out as per plan during winter). This indeed could have been a litmus test of Pakistan's commitment to bilateralism as agreed to in the Shimla agreement.

The peace that followed after the repatriation of the Pak POWs was utilized to advantage by acquiring a deterrent capability against Pak by way of large scale mechanization of the army, thanks to a visionary Gen K Sundarjee at the helm, who bonded well with Arun Singh, MoS for Defence and close to a youthful Rajiv Gandhi as PM. With the highest ever allocation for Defence, close to 3 per cent of the GDP, Indian Army acquired not only tanks, ICVs, Bofors 155mm artillery guns but also was instrumental in the induction into IAF of a very large fleet of MI-8 medium lift helicopters, MI-26, heavy lift helicopters, AN-32 medium lift transport aircrafts and IL-76 heavy lift transports capable of carrying 40 tonnes of combat load. A major reorganisation of the Army's Infantry divisions got underway with greater mechanization and soon Reorganised Plains Infantry Divisions (RAPIDS) took the place of Infantry Divisions in plains. The acquisitions of the transport aircrafts and helicopters gave the army a sizable tactical and strategic lift capability which was exploited to great advantage in meeting two major operational logistics challenges in the years to follow.

Occupation of the Saltoro Ridge and the beginning of the Siachen Conflict

Peace or cold war on the Line of Control (LC), hitherto confined to use of small arms and aggressive patrolling on both sides to gain moral ascendancy by local commanders was in the summer of 1984, disturbed by an unexpected development related to exercise of sovereign rights in allowing passage over territory in the disputed area of J&K.

Taking advantage of the growing interest shown by reputed mountaineers in the world on famous peaks in the Karakorams, like Gasherbrum, Sia Kangri and so on, Pakistan Government encouraged mountaineers to climb these peaks traversing through its side of LC and crossing over passes like SiaLa/ BilafondLa on the Saltoro ridge north of the undelineated portion of the LC in the glacier area. Pakistan also surreptitiously sought to gain a cartographic advantage by extending notionally the Northern most coordinates on the LC at NJ9842 to Karakoram pass eastwards thus obfuscating the status of the un-delineated portion of the LC in the area of the glaciers. Growing wary of Pakistan's intentions, India preempted Pakistani movements East of the Saltoro ridge by occupying the two main passes at Siala and BilafondLa at heights in excess of 20000 ft in early summer of 1984 in a daring helicopter borne operation. Ever since, deployment on the Saltoro ridge line and in depth areas of Siachen glacier has steadily increased on both sides, Pakistan has tried to evict our troops as also occupy portions of the ridge line but has had negligible success.

Siachen has proved yet again the indomitable character of the Indian Army, its ethos summed up by the troika of good leadership, stoical troops and intensive training for the task.

Stand-Off at Wangdung

Having taken steps in modernization to retain a distinct combat edge against Pakistan, in early 1980s the Army set about improving its infrastructure of roads and landing grounds in the Eastern sector extending from Sikkim to Arunachal Pradesh. The Chinese intrusion in the Tawang sector at Wangdung in 1986 threw a direct challenge to the Army. Not since 1967, when there was a face off in Sikkim at Nathu La, that Indian army was tested on a much larger scale by an intrusion across the Line of Actual Control (LAC). The Army accepted the challenge and apart from occupying the heights around the Chinese locality quickly, put into effect its contingency plan for a forward posture deployment opposite Tibet in Arunachal Pradesh and Sikkim.

As mentioned earlier the enhanced logistics capability particularly the availability of MI-8 helicopters (for dropping defence stores as far forward as needed) and combined with AN-32 aircrafts (permitting maintenance of forward troops by air) enabled the Indian Army to upgrade its defence preparedness to such levels as to convince China to wind down its aggressive intent and agree to a more pragmatic non-confrontational border management means to maintain what has come to be called confidence building measures (CBMs). The army's confident posturing on the ground, no doubt helped by adequate air logistics capability provided by the IAF, eventually provided the diplomatic breakthrough in the visit of Rajiv Gandhi, the PM to China and commencement of border talks thereafter.

Commitment in Sri Lanka 'Operation Pawan'

In hindsight and particularly now with the defeat of the LTTE and the killing of its leader Prabhakaran by a resurgent Sri Lankan armed forces, it can be said that the Indian Army's intervention in sending initially a peacekeeping force of a division in support of the Indo-Sri Lanka accord and later expanding the mandate by increasing the commitment to an IPKF (Corps plus) to fight and subdue LTTE and recapture areas held by it in the North and East, was not thought through end to end. While the rapid deployment from Indian mainland was once again facilitated by the availability of air transport support from IAF, however, in rushing troops straight into battle without orientation training and without coordination with own intelligence agencies, the army suffered very heavy casualties in achieving the aim of liberating captured areas in towns and cities from the LTTE and getting it to negotiate for peace with the Sri Lankan Government.

Improvised explosive devices (IEDs), as coined for the first time in the modern military lexicon by the Indian Army (the term now having found universal acceptance due to its large scale usage in Iraq and in Afghanistan by terrorists) were LTTE's main weapon of war and they used it in very innovative ways, having studied Indian Army's individual and small team tactics minutely before their betrayal of the unsuspecting Indian troops. The Indian Army learnt a lot of lessons before returning home after nearly three years of fighting irregular warfare and these were to prove useful later in fighting insurgency in J&K.

Proxy War in J&K and Insurgency in the North East

Emboldened by the close rapport established by its Inter Services Intelligence (ISI) Wing with CIA, in successfully defeating the Soviets by Mujahidin and installing Taliban rule in nearly 90 per cent of Afghanistan by early 1990s, Pakistan, having achieved strategic depth in the West turned towards Indian J&K in launching a fully supported Jihad by stoking anti-India sentiments in the valley initially and later to other parts of the state of J&K.

Rampant unemployment in Pakistan, ever willing indoctrinated youth to die for the cause of Islam on its side and misguided youth on the Indian side helped by a poor and politicised administrative structure of the state of J&K has helped Pakistan sustain the proxy war for nearly two decades. The Indian Army has from the very beginning of infiltration from across the LC faced the challenge squarely, showing utmost restraint in preventing any possibility of collateral damage to unsuspecting/

hapless civilians as also to their property. Showing concern for human rights, the Army follows a set of edicts/commandments issued by its chief that has the appreciation of the Supreme Court and violators of the code of conduct are dealt with examplary by the Army itself. Having raised a separate force to combat insurgency comprising lightly equipped infantry soldiers mixed with a complement of all arms (performing same tasks but drawn proportionately from army other than Infantry to gain experience as also to lessen the commitment of Infantry), Rashtriya Rifles as this Force is called, has acquitted itself well and its organization and deployment in J&K, in the second tier in depth for counter insurgency/counter terrorist tasks permits the rest of the Army to be deployed as per need on the LC for counter-infiltration tasks. What has been unique in the Army's tactics, is the use of minimum force. The Indian Army has completely eschewed use of airpower including any form of even armed helicopters to avoid causing harmful collateral damage. This is unique in the world as it stands in sharp contrast to use of disproportionate force such as use of fighter jets, attack helicopters, combat drones firing missiles by most of the world armies in counter terrorist operations including Pakistan in NWFP, FATA and in Balochistan.

Indian Army's credo of fighting insurgency with an iron fist in velvet gloves as spelt out by one of its former Chiefs, and as a part of a national strategy to go hand in hand with development has been successful in the seven sister states that constitute the North East region. Today due mainly to the Army's relentless campaign right since the 1950s when the Army was deployed to deal with an armed insurrection by underground Nagas with a great deal of support from sanctuaries across the Indian border in Burma as Myanmar was then known, the North East region is home to people who are completely integrated with the rest of India and only a low level of insurgency remains in the state of Manipur and parts of Assam and two districts of Arunachal Pradesh bordering Myanmar. Like in J&K, in the East too the Army has raised a lightly armed and in this case mostly locally recruited force called Assam Rifles, a paramilitary Force, under the home ministry but under Army operational control. The army has in order to continually update its counterinsurgency tactics and provide pre-induction training to newly inducted units established a Counterinsurgency and Jungle Warfare School, which today is being sought after for training by armies of developed nations.

Kargil War Sequel, Operation Parakram, Nuclear Dimension and New Proactive Doctrine

Indian and Pakistan troops had ever since Gen Musharraf's Kargil misadventure in 1999, and India's comprehensive victory over the intruders had been in a state of higher preparedness with higher incidences of small arms and artillery exchanges across the LOC.

During the Kargil war when there was a possibility of escalation of conflict, Pakistan hinted at the possibility of use of nuclear weapons should certain thresholds be crossed if India succeeds in its conventional campaign.

Post the attack on Indian Parliament in December 2001, by Pak terrorists, with India rapidly mobilizing for war, code named Op Parakram, Pakistan responded by similarly mobilizing its troops and once again started using the nuclear blackmail but India silenced it by emphatically referring to its nuclear doctrine of inflicting unacceptable damage should Pakistan resort to first use of a nuclear weapon. Indian gains of keeping Pakistan army deployed for nearly one year as part of its coercive diplomacy have been considerable. First, it shattered Pakistan's bogey of nuclear blackmail. Secondly, it permitted holding of Assembly elections in J&K in 2003 and thirdly, it forced Pakistan to seek a ceasefire on the LOC because it could no longer afford to continue to incur the maintenance cost of continuing the cold war with India, except for the low cost proxy war with terrorists.

The Indian Army having learnt its lesson in Operation Parakram, of being constrained logistically in having to fully mobilize before launch of its strike elements and therefore in not being able to take immediate, credible and telling punitive action against Pakistan in such similar proactive situations that could occur in the future, decided henceforth to adopt a proactive strategy of bringing to bear available forces for an immediate response to any such incident (as decided by the Central govt), and thereafter mobilizing rest of the armed forces for a full-scale war, thus calibrating own response depending on the adversary's reactions. This strategy turned into a doctrine and similarly adapted by the IAF, the Navy and by the Chiefs of Staff for joint operations, has since 2003 been further refined and fitted into an overarching TacC4I system, that the army is likely to be fielding as it modernizes as part of its future growth.

Conclusion

From the aforesaid — Indian Army's track record in facing threats to nation's security, it clearly emerges that in not losing an inch of the territory that it inherited on Independence, the Indian Army has earned the trust of the nation in being reliable, always and every time. So, what then will make our Army invincible. The invincibility can be achieved by (a) imparting rigorous training to fresh cadets (b) creating a spirit of peer emulation, (c) impeccable officer like qualities (OLQ) which qualities will inspire confidence in the juniors who in turn will automatically develop faith in their superiors, (d) quality of weapons, (e) full exposure to the use of these weapons. The defence authorities — military and civil —should always bear in mind that wars are not won by machines but by men behind the machines.

In recent years, the Indian Government has realised the goodwill and professional respect that the Indian Army has been able to command from its counterparts in the neighbourhood and in the region as also from friendly foreign countries. Military diplomacy, as an instrument of the nation's foreign policy is poised to gain greater credibility as the Indian Army grows stronger and modernises itself, to meet future challenges.

Chapter 3

Modernization of Indian Armed Forces: The Future Ahead

*Lt Gen Chandra Shekhar, PVSM, AVSM**

We need to understand that defence modernization must imperatively respond to the prevailing challenges and needs of our country. The technology environment is changing and unless the government shortens the development cycle of new equipment, the armed forces will continue to remain in an operationally disadvantageous situation. In the present strategic scenario, the sources of assured military supplies have dwindled even as the availability of new and alternate sources has added to the complexities of procurement. Added to this is the fact that the environment has become conflict prone and uncertain, with the result that the forces have to be prepared to meet contingencies over a wide spectrum of activity and a large physical area of operation.

---

*The writer retired as Vice Chief of the Staff, Indian Army.

Building Military Capability

The strength, type and structure of the armed forces have to take into account the security environment facing the nation, both conventional as well as the nuclear. There is need to organize the Indian armed forces to fight on two fronts, as our unresolved border with China in the North and North East continues to pose a threat despite an improvement in relations. The long drawn proxy war in J&K and our strained relations with Pakistan are serious challenges facing the nation. India has also to plan for dealing with any threat to its sea coast and island territories. The size and shape of the defence forces have also to take into account the threat to the sea-lanes and its trade routes. The non-state actors and terrorists groups are another factor that need mulling over. The military balance between China and Pakistan given below illustrates comparative military capabilities and the compelling need for India to undertake military modernization:

	China	**India**	**Pakistan**
Defence Budget	$35 Bn	6.5 Bn	$3.3 Bn
Army			
Strength	2,090,000	9,80,000	5,20,000
Tanks	8,500	3,314	2,210
Artillery Guns	14,500	4,175	1,590

Navy	**China**	**India**	**Pakistan**
Strength	2,80,000	55,000	22,000
Submarines	61	17	9
Destroyers	18	6	3
Frigates	36	18	8
Missile Craft	188	25	8
Aircraft Carriers	—	1	—

Air Force	China	India	Pakistan
Strength	4,70,000	1,10,000	45,000
Combat Aircraft	3,740	777	429

The other factors that determine capability are the state of indigenous defence industry and the induction of new technology. It takes time to create military capability. It is not possible to accomplish it in a hurry, in times of war. Financial angle is another important consideration. Affordability and budgetary allocation in view of high costs of military equipment and work force requirements have to be taken into account. The political, economic, technological and strategic factors influence the quality and the speed of defence modernization. In India, the following factors are significant in the area of defence modernization:

1. Geopolitical and geostrategic environment;
2. Economic interests;
3. Technology constraints/imperatives;
4. Social and cultural context.

Need for Modernization

The security challenge facing India is diverse, complex and evolving. Instability in our immediate and extended neighbourhood heightens the threat to our security. What happens in the Indian Ocean, West Asia, Central Asia and Southeast Asia influence Indian strategic thinking? Prime Minister Manmohan Singh during his address to Combined Commanders' Conference in October 2005 observed:

"To meet national security challenge, our strategy has to be based on three broad pillars. First is to strengthen ourselves economically and technologically; second, to acquire adequate defence capability to counter and rebut threats to our security, and the third, to seek partnerships both on the strategic front and on the economic and technological front to widen our policy and developmental options."

Thus introduction of cutting-edge technologies, both in the field of defence and civil, becomes equally important. Even though preference to economic development over military development is normally given, it is possible to proceed simultaneously in both the areas once we have attained a certain level in economic development and capabilities. Defence modernization is a priority for the armed forces; however, priorities at the national level are different because of competing needs of other more important social sectors that need funds for development.

It is not the intention here to review the entire range of military modernization under progress but to highlight a few of the important aspects, which illustrate the existing status of army's modernization. This is as follows:

Strategy for Modernization

Joint Doctrine: A joint military doctrine is necessary to prosecute war and conflicts in all their complexities. Joint doctrine not only gives a common perspective but also provides an authoritative guidance for the armed forces on new military technologies that we may use for future operations. Towards achieving the goals of RMA, the government has formulated and released a Joint Military Doctrine. The doctrinal changes in the army doctrine were a response to changing environment and its experiences after its standoff with Pakistan in Operation Parakram of 2002 and the Kargil conflict. The government conceptualized, formulated and released the doctrine to overcome the delay in mobilization of heavy strike elements. The new doctrine envisages a number of task-oriented integrated battle groups penetrating into adversary's territory from a cold start and executing their assigned tasks quickly within a short span before any international pressure comes up. The air force and naval doctrines both emphasize the strategic reach of their respective services and the need to operate in joint service environment in order to achieve synergies of defence effort. Information technologies are the DNA of the current RMA. In addition, C4I2SR systems form the backbone of the RMA. India is witnessing a boom in IT Sector and its strengths leveraging to impart momentum to enhancing our capabilities in C4I2SR sphere. An overall approach is that, it needs to create an integrated defence communication network. Meanwhile, IAF is in the process of completing a state-of-the art wide area network with adequate bandwidth and redundancies that would give high-speed connectivity to all the entities. Besides, they are setting up an imagery dissemination system that would use the IAF WAN system to ensure that latest UAV imagery and satellite picture are available to the pilots and to other services through digital communication system in real time. This network would also enable merging of information available with different operational areas to present a unified view of operational data. This would improve shared situational awareness and synchronization, which are the pillars of NCW. The Indian Navy was first off the block in achieving high-speed connectivity between shore establishment ships, other naval platforms and even logistics installations. The army has also made strides in net-centric warfare and has already exercised a few of the formations.

Streamlining Defence Procurements

The government carried out defence reforms in 2001 to evolve integrated and joint structures for higher defence organization in order to face the emerging threats and consequently achieve the desired levels of modernization. They update the reforms periodically even as these have achieved some degree of maturity. Formation of HQ Integrated Defence Staff has been instrumental for a joint approach towards building military capability. There is streamlining of defence procurement procedures. These include private sector in defence production, spurring R&D, taking long-term perspective in defence planning and budgeting. In addition, there is qualitative up-gradation of personnel in the armed forces. In addition, there is rationalization of manpower—these were among many of the key defence reforms as recommended by the group of ministers report of 2001. However these need to be implemented fully, as lack of a central policy planning staff and absence of Chief of Defence staff greatly inhibit integrated effort in defence modernization.

Technology Induction

At the present juncture, our armed forces are in transition from industrial age forces to knowledge age forces with a portion being equipped with state-of-the-art weapons. While the army has a larger element of industrial age forces, the navy and the air force, which are more technology intensive forces and less manpower intensive, are much better on the equipment profile. Denial and selected availability of technology are all dependent on international relations. A collaborative approach between the users, DRDO, the industry and foreign vendors is the only option. We must transform our buyer-seller relationship to joint ventures. The HAL aircraft-manufacturing factory with some of the other joint ventures with countries like Israel, Russia and France is undertaking the transfer of technology for various weapon systems. This is the right step from the earlier days of licensed production system. Defence public sector units and DRDO must adopt time bound processes, bold management practices, and scrap the process if it does not conform to a reasonable period, rather than seeking frequent time extension, as shelf life of equipment is becoming shorter by the day due to obsolescence.

Precision Guided Munitions

The government considers precision engagement as one of the most important aspects of the ongoing modernization. In addition, they are strengthening this capability in the armed forces. The benefits of PGMs are well known. Precision weapons are a far more efficient substitute for heavy mass retaliation. They enable concentration of effects from geographically widely dispersed forces, contribute to reduced logistics tail, and help in reducing collateral damage. Therefore, increasing the accuracy and range of our missiles, and acquiring and developing a family of PGMs are receiving greater attention in our armed forces.

However, long ranges of weapon platforms are of no use without complementary matching surveillance, target acquisition, battle damage assessment and weapon guidance capabilities. Therefore, besides ground based and air borne early warning systems, space based assets assume importance for imparting force-multiplication effects to air and surface forces. In addition, space is another area used for communications and navigations and we are in the process of increasing our capabilities in this area too. Aerospace capabilities have a long gestation period. It is necessary to carry out cost-effective replacements and selective up gradation of existing systems. All platforms including transport support aircrafts and helicopters with residual life need up-gradation, along with the weapon systems.

Surveillance and Night vision devices

With the change of battlefield scenario, Indian Army is now equipping itself with the latest state-of-the-art technology and looking for night vision equipments between 3000–5000 in another two years time. There are all indications that the 1.1 million-strong army is going hi-tech in all spheres to turn its troops into fighting machines of the 21st century, complete with the latest multi-function weaponry and uniforms with sensors to monitor their health indicators. This can substantially change the battlefield requirement of the army and night fighting profile. It has a tactical advantage for our forces that cannot only enhance their night fighting skills but also improve surveillance and reconnaissance capabilities greatly, but the numbers is large and requires time for induction. Army feels that the night vision equipment will enhance combat potential to facilitate operations over the 24 hours cycle. As a part of its modernization and upgrading weaponry, Indian Army has planned to equip all its battalions with night vision equipments but the progress is painfully slow.

MBT- Arjun Tank Production

The inordinate delay in the production of the ARJUN Tank and its design faults is a major cause of worry. Indian Defence Minister AK Antony has admitted that frequent design modifications and assembling format have also caused additional delay in its induction. His assurance that they are taking necessary steps to ensure the timely availability of all critical aggregates is still far from the reality. The MoD repeats his assurances at regular intervals to justify the public-sector defence undertakings and to secure uninterrupted financial grants. Meanwhile, we continue to import the Russian T-90 and T-72 tanks.

Air Defence Missile System

The recent trials of the surface-to-air missile have accepted Akash, an integral component of a family of missiles envisaged in the Integrated Guided Missile Development Programme of the mid-80s, as a viable weapons platform to form part of an air defence shield over vital Indian installations and cities. This represents a progressive improvement in indigenous expertise in missile technology. Yet there are miles to go before a fail-safe anti-ballistic missile (ABM) system comes into being. It is essential to develop an anti-missile system in view of Pakistan's stated national policy of "First Use" of nuclear weapons. The Akash surface-to-air missile (SAM) is yet only capable of intercepting aircraft and missiles up to a range between 25–30 kilometers. This is, by itself, a creditable achievement by the Defence Research and Development Organization (DRDO). Nevertheless, it needs to make rapid improvements in range to shift from its present capability of being a credible shield against conventional high-explosive warheads to being an anti-ballistic missile (ABM). The air-defence capabilities, sensors, and support systems need a beef up, given the position of the combat squadrons that are dwindling.

Modernization of field Artillery (155mm guns)

As part of the field artillery modernization programme, Indian army issued global tenders (RFP) for the purchase of 400, 155 mm towed artillery guns. The domestic manufacture of 1100 guns that will cost roughly two billion US dollars will come after the imported artillery guns. The scandals and pressures have so upset the artillery modernization programme that the army is even considering buying 130 mm guns as a desperate measure.

This is the third time that the ministry of defence has issued RFP for the howitzer guns. In February 2006, the Indian Army had issued RFP for 140 ultra light howitzers for about US $ 750 million and 180 wheeled self-propelled guns costing US $ 1.2 Billion. The army wants to start the induction process of these guns from 2011–12, as it would take at least five years to equip all the units after the contract is finalized. Because of the scandals and pressures, the project planners had delayed the project due to blacklisting of the concerned firms, which were to supply these.

Pinaka Multiple Barrel Rocket launcher: The Indian Army indigenously developed Pinaka multiple barrel rocket launcher developed by the DRDO. They released Pinaka to the Indian Army. The Ordnance Factory will supply 300 Pinaka Rockets to the army in the first year, and 1,000 rockets in 2009. Pinaka includes the applications on wheeled, tracked and rail vehicles to static ground based mounts all the way to ship-borne platforms.

BrahMos Cruise Missile: Russia-India joint venture Brahmos Aerospace Private Limited, founded in 1998, is engaged in developing and manufacturing supersonic anti-ship cruise missile meant for land to-land and sea-to-land attack role although its air-to-land variant with extended range is under development. The partners in this enterprise named in honour of symbolic "merge" of the rivers Brahmaputra and Moscova, are Defence Research & Development Organization (DRDO) from India and the Federal State Unitary Enterprise NPO Mashinostroyenia (NPOM) from Russia. The missile can be launched either in a vertical or inclined position over a 360degree horizon.

Indigenous Defence Production

For self-reliance, an excellent defence manufacturing industry is a necessary pre-condition. The planners have streamlined our defence procurement procedures and policies to encourage private and foreign participation in defence industrial sector. The objectives are to achieve synergy between civil and government sectors by integrating their capabilities. Technological and science skills, management capabilities and ability of civil sectors to raise resources would let R & D capabilities of government laboratories and institutions to produce state-of-the-art defence equipment. Further, direct offsets in defence industries against procurement from foreign sources will encourage the transfer of technology and investments from abroad.

Budgetary Support

The budgetary constraints would dictate the future direction and pace of modernization. Presently, the budget is at very modest levels of 2.3 per cent of the GDP. Even in current five years defence plan (2007–12), the defence budget is likely to be around 2.5 per cent of the GDP. If there is a sustained growth of eight per cent and above in the economy, then it may be possible to allot additional budget for the defence. Currently, and in the next five-year plan there would be added emphasis on technologies, equipment and strategies to counter terrorism as also to create a credible deterrence capability. Surveillance, communication equipment and sensors would be major areas for development and acquisition. Cyber security and achieving synergy in the field of information technology would continue to be the focus of modernization. However, a long-term perspective, accountability in decision-making, a firm financial commitment and fast-track procurements procedure will be mandatory to ensure significant military capability.

Conclusion

It is evident that the state of our defence modernization is unsatisfactory and there is urgent need for drastic institutional measures. We are yet to buy a single artillery gun in 23 years. We have an aging naval fleet and dwindling numbers of advance jet fighters. Therefore, there is a compelling need to give it a great impetus. India also has a bitter experience of foreign vendors not fulfilling their contractual commitments once these vendors receive their payments. They fail to provide accepted after-sale support; besides, they jack up the cost of spares, and decline to honour transfer of technology. India's failure to negotiate foolproof contracts has allowed Russia to increase the cost of aircraft carrier Gorshkov manifolds. Similar contractual flaws have resulted in delays in the deliveries of Hawk trainers, T-90 tanks kits, and Scorpene submarines. It is essential that we develop critical technologies ourselves or enter joint ventures with strategic partners. We also need to have professional teams to negotiate defence contracts. This would need establishing a dedicated procurement agency staffed by professionals, who are experts and are accountable to the defence minister directly.

References

FORCE, Vol 7, Oct 2009 pp. 8-9 'Challenges and Opportunities', ACM FH Major, 2. and Security News, p. 4.

2. USI-CIISS Seminar Report, Sep 06, pp.21-24 'Revolution in Military Affairs'.
3. Strategic Affairs, Vol 2 Issue 7, March 08, pp.17 and 37.
4. Strategic Affairs, Vol 2 Issue 5, Jan 08, pp. 5-7.

Chapter 4

Strategy for Employment of Special Forces

*Lt General PC Katoch, UYSM, AVSM, SC**

Turmoil describes the world today, especially in our immediate neighbourhood. The Americans are terming the global situation by the acronym VUCA (Volatile, Uncertain, Complex, and Ambiguous). In this fluid geostrategic environment, conflict situations show clear trends that irregular or asymmetric forces have emerged with greater strategic value than nuclear or conventional forces, highlighting a distinct disadvantage to India; conventional responses to asymmetric threats are impotent.

---

*The writer is a retired Director-General, Information Systems of the Indian Army and erstwhile Colonel of the Special Forces and Parachute Regiment.

How are we coping with transnational and non-traditional challenges to our security? Following a comprehensive review of national security post-Kargil conflict, the National Security Council and office of the National Security Advisor were set up in 1999. Recent additions have been a Multi-Agency Centre and the National Investigation Agency (NIA). Yet, tremendous work needs to be done to streamline our national security including inter-agency coordination and to evolve a national strategy for employment of special forces commensurate with our national interests.

India's Neighbourhood

China continues to consolidate her comprehensive national power, emerging as a major player in the world order. Her peace facade is backed by the 'Doctrine of Pre-emption and Surprise' that encompasses surprise, deception and shock. Modernization of Chinese armed forces is ominous, not only along the Tibetan border but also in the Indian Ocean Region (IOR). We see a more assertive China now flexing her muscles across the IOR and Asia-Pacific with scant regard to Vietnam, Indonesia, Malaysia, Brunei and Philippines, unilaterally extending her maritime boundaries in the South China Seas. China wants the IOR to be recognised as a Chinese sphere of influence, managed by Chinese nuclear submarines and carriers. Her strategic designs for control of the IOR can be appreciated with her footprints in Seychelles to dominate even the western limit of the Indian Ocean. Not only does she have the biggest embassy in Seychelles, she has built refuelling facilities in the outlying islands of Seychelles and has an agreement with them for their use by China, Seychelles and their friends. She occupies 38,000 square kilometre of our territory in Aksai Chin not only to give depth to the Western Highway but more significantly for the oil reserves that are rumoured to be there. She claims entire Arunachal Pradesh as "South Tibet" and sniggers at India's development and approach to neighbours. When China says she can wait for 100 years to take over Taiwan, we should expect a similar approach to the so called "South Tibet".

The US assessed a decade ago that China will start flexing her military muscle from 2010 onwards. It obviously will act southwards; India and Bhutan, with whom she has deliberately not settled her borders. Chinese claims to Arunachal are not merely to deflect attention from mainland Tibet issue but indicate her resolve to reach the warm waters of the Indian Ocean through as many land routes as possible. That is the reason for her urge to take the railway through the Karakoram to Pakistan and the transportation corridor through Myanmar. That is the reason China claims the Doklam Plateau in Bhutan; to get a clear run through the Siliguri Corridor. This threat is extremely serious if seen in conjunction with Maoists of Nepal and Maoist-Naxalite fault line in India, especially if the Maoists of Nepal gain total control of Nepal in coming years. Perhaps China needs to be reminded of the Kushan dynasty; empires of Chandragupt Maurya and Ashoka the Great that had parts of China under them and that not very far back Indian Army was garrisoned at Yatung. Perhaps she needs to be educated on the research by John Man chronicled in his book Kublai Khan, that in 7th Century the Kingdom of Tibet was much bigger than China and that in 763, Tibet had even captured the then capital of China.

China is racing ahead full steam with an "Encircle India" policy (Chinese String of Pearls) in an innocuous manner. She has developed military relations with all countries around India and has transferred nuclear technology to Pakistan. Her port construction and other activities in Myanmar, Pakistan, Maldives, Mauritius and Seychelles are noteworthy. She is already linked with Pakistan by road, Tibet by road and rail, and plans to extend the railway to Pakistan and Sikkim. Her transportation corridor through Myanmar is well underway. In all probability she is manipulating the Maoists of Nepal to her advantage including through them the Maoist/Naxalite movement in India. According to a report published in the DEBKA files in 2002, "The Maoist insurgency in Nepal may be one of the last surviving operations of a little known Chinese intelligence organ known as the Ministry of Foreign Liaison, a body of CCP set up in Mao Zedong time. Chinese intelligence infiltration operations into Nepal, that began decades ago, set off a self-perpetuating Maoist "People's War" that has never really ended. It would be in China's interests to install a regime in Kathmandu that is not too friendly with the US or India." This has profound consequences for India. As per a retired IB official, China has been known to be training Naga, Mizo and other north-east insurgents in the Paoshan area of southern China. Paresh Barua, ULFA chief, too reportedly has shifted his base and training camps to Chinese territory. The article by Zhan Lue, so-called Chinese strategist recommending China should splinter India into 20-30 independant nation states needs to be viewed in this context. Even more significant is the fact that such an article was published in the journal of the Institute of Strategic Studies that has Chinese government backing. Chinese policy towards India lately is "no holds barred"; safeguarding Azhar Masood of JeM from being labelled a terrorist, pumping fake drugs as 'Made in India' into Africa and flooding fake currency into India courtesy Pakistan.

China probably has the most extensive cyber warfare capability in the world and willingness to use it more aggressively than any other country. Notorious for her "botnets" and "bot" armies, she is known to be engaged in cyber attacks globally. She has already demonstrated the capability to shoot down satellites. These capabilities of China should be of profound concern to us.

Pakistan continues on the farcical legacy of Musharraf declaring to the international media as President of Pakistan that "there is no terrorist on Pakistani soil". The same Musharraf, who as an SSG officer was training terrorists in Chittagong Hill Tracts in 1971. The same Musharraf, who as Army Chief stooped the lowest during Operation Vijay in not accepting the bodies of his own martyred soldiers. Even the *Dawn* published from Karachi reported that over five hundred bodies of the then

Northern Light Infantry soldiers were dumped unceremoniously at their door steps in POK in the middle of the night without any military honour — obviously on orders of Musharraf. The same Musharraf, who as President of Pakistan in his autobiography alludes to India as the "most devious enemy" repeatedly. The same Musharraf, who was befittingly given a shut up call during the last *India Today* Conclave in Delhi by Maulana Mahmood Madani, Member of Rajya Sabha. Yet the fools that we are, we keep referring to Musharraf, as the 'best bet'.

Zardari's admission of Pakistan having nurtured militancy and extremism as a policy has little cause for glee since his civilian government is a puppet against the ISI-Pakistan Army combine and dominant mullahs. The Jihad Factory in Pakistan is running full steam. Nasir Abbas Mirza wrote in *Daily Time* of Pakistan on 11 May 2009, "There are thousands of madrassas spread all over Pakistan's urban centres that are producing millions of neo-drones… Take a little boy teach him about the fanciful world that awaits him in the heaven and that in order to attain that he has to destroy everything that stands in his way, including his own body... At full steam ahead in Pakistan, this is a monstrous experiment in brainwashing and it is on a par with, if not worse than, Nazi Germany's eugenics. They did it in the name of science; here, it is being done in the name of God and religion. On a very large scale, this is a hugely successful experiment in which nurture triumphs and nature takes a beating". The author goes on to say that no politician in Pakistan can dare raise his voice against the mullahs.

Pakistan has not banned the al-Qaeda, continues to drag investigations of Mumbai massacre without punishing those involved and has linked curbing the LeT with purported Indian interference in Balochistan. The Pakistan Army and the ISI continue their double game in Swat; providing havens and support to Afghan Taliban leadership in Quetta and tribal areas of NWFP while acting against the Pakistani Pakhtuns who support the Afghan population. Taliban influence is spreading to Punjab province of Pakistan. Danger of Pakistan seeking to divert attention by escalating terrorist violence in India is real. Taliban linkages with al-Qaeda, insurgents in our North East and Maoists/Naxalites throw up further challenges for our security.

Sincerity of the Pakistani Army in operations against the Taliban in Swat is highly questionable. A Peshawar based journalist when interviewed by the *Dawn* in June this year on Pakistani Army's operations in Swat, replied whether anyone had ever killed his golden hen. According to him, the Taliban is the golden hen of the Pakistan Army, providing them strategic depth. An ex DG of ISI has stated in an open forum that Pakistan has the wherewithal to Balkanize India and will continue to do so. Kargil should be seen as continuation of the unalterable objective of Pakistan to forcibly wrest Kashmir from India. Newly commissioned Pakistani officers while passing out from the officer's academy at Kakul still take an oath to avenge the loss of East Pakistan. As long as the stakes of a conflict stay below the level of vital interests of India, Pakistan may be able to manipulate the terms of engagement. Already, Pakistan is waging an asymmetric war against India, using terrorism / proxy war, drug trafficking, financial war (injecting fake Indian currency and trying to target financial institutions through terrorists), psychological war (attempt targeting Indian Military Academy by proxy to worsen officer shortages), information war (hackers). As part of psychological warfare, ISI may also be using the fourth estate in India to demoralise the Indian military including hampering modernisation plans. A former Joint Secretary of the Intelligence Bureau states in his book, "The susceptibility of the fourth estate to the intelligence community had tied our hands down. They are one of the too many holy Indian cows. Some of them, as described by a senior member of the fourth estate, 'taxi on hire' any paymaster can hire this particular brand."

According to the book *From a Head, through a Head, to Head* published in Karachi in 2000, "Zhou Enlai suggested to Ayub Khan that Pakistan should prepare for a prolonged conflict with

India instead of short-term wars. He advised Pakistan to raise a Militia Force to act behind enemy lines". Pakistan has raised this Militia in the form of Jihadis. A retired IB official states, "Way back in 1992-93... the process of 'transplanting armed modules' in the heartland of India had started taking cognizable shape". Pakistan's proxy war aims are strategic and wider in scope. The intentions are not Kashmir specific. It emerges from a smaller nation's strategy of bleeding a major adversary through asymmetric warfare. She stands emboldened to bleed and strategically taunt India due to a combination of factors like India's inability and restraint in not countering Pakistani designs effectively, nuclear blackmail and collusion with China.

Unfortunately for us, US-Pakistan mutual dependency will remain critical viz-a-viz US-India needs in strategic and security values, at least in short and midterms, especially till US presence remains in Afghanistan, unless a major event alters this equation. This is an undeniable fact that India must acknowledge.

Democracy in Nepal is a welcome development but the degree of influence wielded by the Maoists and their approach to governance will decide the future of peace and stability. Presence of PLA in Nepal whether as construction workers or manning three star hotels run by Chinese should not be discounted. Chinese links to the Maoists in Nepal and through them, their links with the Maoists in India need to be observed closely. It is also prudent not to forget Pushpa Kamal Dahal alias Prachanda's statement to the Nepalese media in 2001 that "The ultimate war will be with the Indian Army". Recent reports that Prachanda is trying to become the head of an international Maoist organisation and his statements that US and India have been planning to attack China from Nepalese territory need to be viewed seriously, especially with the developing left wing extremist movement in India.

Bhutan is our most peaceful and stable neighbour and has undergone peaceful transition to democracy. However, mishandling of the Bhutanese issue can have adverse impact for India. The geo-strategic location of Myanmar is of great consequence to India. It not only shares a long border with both India and China but also flanks the Bay of Bengal to the East. Bereft of a democratically elected government, the country has been ruled by the Military Junta with pronounced pro-China leanings. Amid world pressure the Junta has found a willing ally in China. Should China succeed in establishing naval bases in Myanmar, it will have enormous consequences on India's naval dominance in the Bay of Bengal, as also the situation in our North East states and Bangladesh.

In Bangladesh, though the Awami League government is traditionally India friendly, the continuing problem of illegal migration and the emergence of radical groups in Bangladesh which support terrorist attacks, ISI nexus and Bangladesh's close military relations with China are a cause of concern. Asymmetric capabilities of Bangladesh need monitoring as intentions can change overnight. It is significant to note that even Sheikh Mujibur Rehman authoring a book prior to liberation of Bangladesh wrote, "Because Eastern Pakistan must have sufficient land for expansion, Eastern Pakistan must include Assam to be financially and economically strong". We need to be wary of a future Chinese push from the North, through the Siliguri corridor, to attempt reaching the warm waters of the Indian Ocean, especially at a time when a China friendly government is ruling Bangladesh.

In Sri Lanka the LTTE has been defeated. However there is a huge humanitarian crisis looming large with scores of Tamil refugees who were caught in the crossfire and now are virtually homeless. Until a credible devolution package by the Sri Lankan Government and a final political settlement to the issue is put in place, the threat of a resurgence of extremism will remain. Growing influence of China and Pakistan in Sri Lanka at this critical juncture must be closely observed. Chinese offer to refit Sri Lankan Navy and assist Sri Lanka in building port facilities etc is not without reason.

Maldives is looking towards deepening relations with India. However, there is a need to simultaneously monitor the increasing Chinese influence in Maldives as also the influence of al-Qaeda-Taliban-Pakistan sponsored radicals. It is also significant to note that during the last anti-India wave in a small country like Fiji, exodus of hundreds of Indian businessmen saw a quiet influx of an equal number of Chinese businessmen. Our 'Look East Policy' has resulted not only in stable and strong economic and trade relations with South East Asia but also bringing into focus security of Sea Lanes of Communications (SLsOC) as a major common concern.

Challenges for India

India faces multifarious threats and challenges, the key ones being related to terrorism, border management and maritime security. The Indian dilemma includes conventional and nuclear threats, asymmetric threats including terrorism, failed / failing states in our neighbourhood, and demographic assault. India has become home to the largest number of domestic terrorist organisations, 27 numbered by MHA in June 2009 and the Maoists have created the biggest fault line in India affecting 180 districts in 17 States. These terror organisations are exploitable by China/Pakistan's-ISI/al-Qaeda/Taliban/LeT; to form groupings and establish a compact revolutionary zone. While infiltration, illegal migration and demographic assault continue unabated, Talibanisation of Pakistan would pose further threats to India's security. In the North East, insurgents exploit porous borders and enjoy the luxury of safe havens in neighbouring countries. Similarly, infiltration continues unabated in J&K. Of course, porosity of borders cannot be one way and can be exploited from both sides.

The Indian Ocean Region has assumed great importance due to sheer magnitude of international trade that transits between the Straits of Hormuz and the Malacca Straits. This makes the region important not only for India but the entire world. Hijackings by pirates have brought into sharp focus the pivotal role that India can play in securing these SLsOC. India needs to secure its numerous island territories as well as offshore assets related to hydrocarbon fuels. In addition to its maritime boundary of 7683 kilometres, India shares a land border of approximate 15,000 kilometres with six countries viz Pakistan, Bangladesh, China, Nepal, Bhutan and Myanmar. Despite attempts to improve border management by use of latest technology, problems persist. Continuing illegal migration from Bangladesh has resulted in alteration of the demographic balance in the North East, causing major strife in the region. In the West, the border-fence has curbed the problem of narcotics smuggling to a large extent. However infiltration attempts continue in J&K due to the inherent problems of sealing the borders in an inhospitable terrain.

Notwithstanding the periodic exuberance displayed through Hindi - Chini or Hindi - Pakistani Bhai - Bhai slogans, we should accept in our national interest that our adversaries will relentlessly seek ways to mitigate India's power and status through asymmetric warfare. When Musharraf spoke of many more Kargils, he certainly did not imply conventional wars.

Role of Special Forces

Special Forces have wide applications across the entire spectrum of conflict, more so as a controlled response along the escalatory ladder in the emerging strategic environment. Not a mere tactical tool, they have ample scope of employment to face challenges of terrorism, information, asymmetric and NBC warfare. According to Stephen Cohen, "The task of Special Forces is the proxy application of force at low and precisely calculated levels, the objective being to achieve some political effect, not a battlefield victory." While Special Forces should be central to asymmetric response, asymmetric warfare does not equate automatically to a physical attack. A physical attack is only the extreme and potentially most dangerous expression of asymmetric warfare. The key lies in achieving strategic objectives through application of modest resources with the essential psychological component.

Force Projection by Indian Special Forces has only been undertaken once as part of the IPKF. The ideal response to asymmetric threats is adoption of a proactive strategy ensuring prevention of any attack against Indian assets / national interests. This strategy appears to be missing in our context. A retired Intelligence Bureau official writes in his book, "I continued to advocate for an aggressive and proactive counter and forward intelligence thrust against Pakistan. My voice was rarely heard and mostly ignored." He further states, "The Pakistani establishment is a geopolitical bully. The best response to blunt such a bully is to take the war inside his home. India has allowed itself to be blackmailed by Pakistan even before it went nuclear. The sabre rattling of coercive diplomacy, which is nothing but sterile military power, cannot convince the Islamist Pakistani establishment that India can take the border skirmishes inside their homes and hit at the very roots of the jaundiced Islamic groups."

Special Forces are strategic assets and should not be wasted on tactical tasks. The Germans employed pseudoteams in Ardennes in World War II. The British employed pseudoteams against communist guerrillas and in Kenya against the Mau-Mau insurgents. SAS is presently operating in Iraq, Afghanistan and some African countries. Selous Scouts raised in Rhodesia in 1973 were responsible for 68 per cent of all terrorists killed in the next six years of Bush War at cost of only 40 Scouts. Russia's Spetsnaz are currently entrenched in CIS and Eastern bloc countries in one form or another. US Special Forces (USSF) were employed in Afghanistan and in Iraq since year and a half prior to the invasion and are still inside Iraq. In 2007, USSF was operating in some 186 countries, though fighting only in Afghanistan and Iraq. Like the SSG, we need to understand that Special Forces do not create resistance movements but advice, train and assist resistance movements already in existence.

Core tasks that foreign Special Forces have been undertaking are direct action, special reconnaissance, foreign internal defence, unconventional warfare, counterterrorism, counterproliferation of WMDs, civil affairs operations, psychological operations and information operations. Some of the tasks that US Special Forces undertake are as under:-

- Conduct proactive, sustained "man hunting" and disruption operations globally.
- Build partner capacity in relevant ground, air and maritime capabilities in scores of countries on a steady — state basis.
- Help generate persistent ground, air and maritime surveillance and strike coverage over "under-governed" areas and littoral zones.
- Employ unconventional warfare against state sponsored terrorism and transnational terrorist groups globally.

Despite the above tasks undertaken by US Special Forces in their own national interest, no one accuses them of terror. This needs to be understood by our mandarins who may go ballistic at the thought of our Special Forces employed to control fault lines of our adversaries.

While globally, Special Forces are looking outwards, we have confined our Special Forces within the country save the sole IPKF experience. Gen Padmanabhan, a former Chief of the Indian Army, in 2001 went on record to say, "India's Special Forces are ill-equipped and underutilized."

Indian Special Forces

Combined strength of the Indian Special Forces is already in the region of 18,000 and plans are afoot for further expansions. This includes Special Forces of the three Services, National Security Guard (NSG) and the Special Frontier Force (SFF). This combined strength is much more than the uniformed strength of total USSF but not one tenth their capabilities. According to the CGS of Special Operations Command (SOCOM) of the US, even in the peak period of Special Forces deployment in Iraq, only 90 x Operation Detachments Alpha (ODAs) were actually used (each ODA is 10-12 strong). Incidentally, SOCOM presently is only 13,000 strong of which psychological operations teams and civil affairs teams are not fighting men. Expansion has been very deliberate in case of foreign special forces.

Post 9/11, the US expanded its Special Forces only by 750 commencing 2008. UK went in only for an addition of a 650 strong "Special Forces Support Group". Pakistan has added a fourth SSG unit only recently. With three SSG units they were able to wreak havoc in Afghanistan, J&K, Bangladesh and Nepal. In contrast, we have gone in for rapid expansion of our Special Forces ignoring the following globally accepted SF Truths:

- Humans are more important than hardware.
- Quality is better than quantity.
- Special Forces cannot be mass produced.
- Competent Special Forces cannot be created after emergencies arise.

Recent uncorroborated reports that Pakistan's SSG is expanding to a Division sized force appears a deliberate plan to accelerate the mad rush of Special Forces expansion in India and make us lose the focus in the bargain. It is highly unlikely that while SSG took 20 years to add the fourth SSG battalion, now suddenly is expanding to division strength. Incidentally, a trained soldier volunteer for the SSG has to undergo nine months of probation-cum-continuation training before he can wear the SSG beret. By rapidly expanding our Special Forces we have actually diluted their capabilities; sans requisite manpower, training, weapons and equipment and are playing into the very gameplan of the asymmetric adversary.

The NSG was originally conceived as a 25,000 strong force and the army was supposed to contribute manpower only for the first 10 years. Growth of the NSG remained stunted due to lack of foresight and now we want to expand them overnight. Perception is obviously lacking in differentiating between raising a police / para military force and a special force. It is not possible to create special forces within 6-8 months whether in NSG or the military. Observing our response of rapid expansion of the NSG and army special forces getting sucked into the national counterterrorism grid, we should expect more 26/11 type terror attacks on targets away from this grid deployment. Pakistan will like to ensure that our Special Forces get fully embroiled domestically.

Employment

The Special Forces are Strategic Assets and their tasking should be in furtherance of national interests. They should undertake high risk, and high gain missions having minimum visibility with desired effect. They should be employed to continuously 'shape the battlefield' throughout the conflict spectrum including asymmetric and fourth generation wars, complementing conventional forces.

Tasks

The deteriorating situation in our neighbourhood, increasing asymmetric threats and national security challenges have blurred the dividing line between subconventional and conventional wars coupled with cyber threats and possibility of use of dirty bombs and gas / chemical attacks by terrorists. Security is a challenge to stay, as it is dynamic and manifests into new forms. The threat today, is to a nation as a whole in order to cripple it, the objectives therefore include the infrastructure – railways, national power grid, national information grid, aviation, surface transport, nuclear / atomic centres, financial institutions and their networks, defence installations and their networks, monuments and installations of national significance, diplomatic enclaves etc. At the same time we should ensure that our Special Forces look primarily beyond our borders to nip the asymmetric threats in the bud and to control the fault lines of our adversaries. Their tasking should include responding to trans-national asymmetric, unconventional and fourth generation threats, special operations, reconnaissance, psychological operations, counterproliferation and the like.

Intelligence

Intelligence is the key to security. Acquisition, collation and timely dissemination of intelligence are a major grey area which has been repeatedly highlighted during various crisis situations including the 26/11 attacks in Mumbai. The security apparatus is plagued by lack of inter-agency coordination. We lack a single permanent organisation at the apex. Provision of continuous intelligence inputs to our Special Forces from national intelligence agencies needs to be institutionalised. We do not have an effective national information grid and this really should not wait for completion of the National Power Grid, which would take considerable time. We need to establish the means for automated intelligence gathering and analysis, continuous assessments (short, medium and long term) supported by an automated decision support system, and finally real time on-line dissemination of the common operating picture accessible by concerned agencies. Information technologies exist to do all this. In a state of asymmetric war, of which we are in the midst, such requirements are paramount at the national level and do not concern the military alone. We need to remember that an asymmetric war is waged against a nation and not against the military alone. It requires a national response.

Inter-Agency Coordination

Employment of Special Forces, particularly in asymmetric and fourth generation war scenarios, requires tremendous inter-agency coordination. Such coordination is difficult in a democracy like ours given the Indian ego and ethos —

remember the crab story? The only office that can ensure this is that of the prime minister. In any event, employment of Special Forces in response to asymmetric and fourth generation wars would require the express sanction of the prime minister as in the case of US where the president authorises such actions.

Way Ahead

Special Forces provide us the tools to address non-traditional challenges to our security by providing a silent and effective medium to achieve our security objectives. However, the success and effectiveness of special operations can be multiplied manifold by the formulation of a well worked out strategy for their employment. Establishment of a streamlined command and control structure, streamlining the lines of authority, secure and seamless communication links, enhanced inter-agency coordination for intelligence gathering and sharing and establishment of a national Inter-agency database for intelligence are some of the steps that will assist rapid decision making and a coherent response to non-traditional challenges to our security. Special Forces are a vital element of national power possessing capability of enormous freedom of action in methodology of execution of assigned operations and should be fruitfully employed to successfully meet any challenge. As the way ahead, we need to urgently consider the following:

- Install a Special Forces Cell ("Brain") in the Prime Minister's Office to evolve a national doctrine and strategy for strategic employment of Special Forces, oversee their manning, equipping, training, consolidation, operational and intelligence inputs, inter-agency synergy and strategic tasking.

- Establish a single apex organisation for continuous intelligence gathering from all sources (linked to the "Brain" besides others) with automated analysis and assessment (short, medium and long term), supported by an automated decision support system and real time on line dissemination along with the common operating picture to all concerned.

- Establish an effective National Information Grid (NIG), using available Information technology duly linked to the Global Information Grid and all concerned including the Military.
- Ensure that military special forces and the special frontier force look primarily outwards in response to trans-national asymmetric and fourth generation warfare threats.
- Special Groups of NSG and SFF (all being regular Army personnel on deputation) be merged with or placed under the command of Army Special Forces (similar to placing Coast Guard under the command of Navy), and army be tasked for anti-hijack tasks.
- Special Ranger Groups of NSG be expanded and given full responsibility of anti-terrorism tasks instead of providing only outer cordons.
- Ensure expansion of Special Forces is controlled at the apex and planned only after consolidation of existing assets.
- Consider establishment of a tri-service special forces command for special forces of the three Services.
- Consider bringing special forces for home land security under a single headquarter.
- Commence joint training of all special forces, particularly joint operations training between Army Special Forces and the Special Frontier Force.
- Undertake periodic nation-wide anti-terrorism drills using complete security establishments including military without prior warnings.
- Regularise the Special Frontier Force.

It is reiterated that while special forces should be central to response to non-traditional challenges, this does not equate automatically to a physical attack. The key lies in achieving strategic objectives through application of modest resources with the essential psychological component. For this, we need a well thought out coordinated proactive approach. Diplomacy and conventional war cannot contend with asymmetric wars of Pakistan and China. The perception during 1989-1992 was that low intensity conflict in J&K was a valley problem; limited to north of Banihal and west of Zojila. How it has expanded and how much of the defence establishment it has sucked needs little elaboration.

As a nation we must understand that if we continue to follow a defensive mentality, the asymmetric adversary / adversaries will tie us up in knots; playing cat and mouse, adversely affecting our economic growth and well being. Merely fortressing one's house in asymmetric war situations is not enough. Defensive-reactive mentality in non-traditional conflict situations amounts to cowardice. In this context, it is significant to note what Mahatma Gandhi once said, "If one has to choose between cowardice and violence, I will choose violence" (as told to Lt Gen LP Sen – then Commander Designate 191 Infantry Brigade in 1947). Choices with us are to go in for proactive defence in this asymmetric war or continue bleeding through 2000 cuts; 1000 each courtesy Pakistan (ISI/LeT/JeM/Jihadis) and China (Maoists/ Naxalites/ULFA etc) while al-Qaeda and Taliban lurk around the corner. We have to cope with asymmetric adversaries ourselves. In such a war, we should not hope for anything globally beyond sympathy. It is time we use our special forces as true strategic assets.

Chapter 5

Internal Security Challenges and Military Power

*Lt General DB Shekatkar, PVSM, AVSM, VSM**

If we compute the total number of days, (between declaration of war which India was forced to fight and the declaration of ceasefire when the war officially terminated) in the history of independent India, till 10 July 2009; the total duration would not be more than 143 days. It means our armed forces specially the army fought conventional wars for little less than six months. If we examine the deployment, employment, direct/indirect involvement of Indian Army in internal security, internal conflicts, namely counter insurgency, counterterrorism, control of communal violence and so on, it comes to almost four decades.

---

*The writer is a Member, Governing Council Centre for Advanced Strategic Studies, Pune.

While the constitutionally defined and assigned principle role of Indian Armed Forces is to protect India from external threats and aggression, protect our territorial integrity and security; there exists a provision to employ the armed forces in internal security (IS) duties to meet IS threats under exceptional circumstances and situations. The operative words of constitutional provision are "Government of India may use the armed forces ..." Since internal security is not the primary role of the armed forces, their services be sought only in rare cases where other security forces and agencies have failed or proved ineffective to address the problem and effectively handle the emerging situation. The qualifying words are "may" and "exceptional circumstances". But thanks to the wisdom and authority of the authorities who interpret and misinterpret the rules as per their wisdom, have replaced the word "may employ" with "will employ" and the words and concepts of "exceptional circumstances" have been replaced (though unofficially, but in practice) with "any circumstance/situation which the authorities feel appropriate". This has resulted in excessive deployment of army in internal security duties over years. Our experience over the years and the realty on ground has proved that there is nearly a permanent deployment of army in managing internal security. Some elements from navy and air force also support the army in internal security. There is an uncontrollable temptation to involve the army at the slightest pretext.

One of the reasons for the frequent call for army's deployment in internal security is the overconfidence among the bureaucrats (who at time wrongly advise and misguide the political masters) that once called for, the army will somehow or the other manage the problem. It is another matter as to what will be the aftereffects and implications of such employment to the nation and army. There is also a "studious awareness" that in case things go wrong due to such frequent employment of army in internal security; none of the policy formulators and decision makers will ever be made answerable or accountable.

As per Carl Van Clausewitz the philosophy and object of war is influenced and decided by politics. His strategic thinking resulted in his famous quote "War is continuation of politics by other means". It is therefore reasonable to assume that there is a close link between politics and war. If researched and analysed carefully same would to some extent hold good in the context of internal conflicts which challenge the internal security environment and use of military power in managing IS environment. Narrow, momentary political interests of a few so- called politicians and political parties in their desire and attempt to challenge the authority of established government create an internal security environment, where in temptations to use military power is difficult to resist. With the changing perspective of warfare and increasing shift towards asymmetrical, unconventional warfare, the military power will increasingly be used within the geographical limits of a nation and within the society as opposed to wars which were fought on the borders or across the borders and away from society. To avoid collateral damage to civilian population and property there were a conscious attempts to fight war away from the society. But this may not hold good in future to come. The conflicts internally errupted or externally supported, will have to be resolved with in the nation and with the involvement of society; hence there will be restriction on use of military power/ combat power in internal security.

While discussing internal security challenges and military power, an important aspect is that of conflicts in various countries of region and its impact on India. India is a major constituent of South Asia which is a region of inbuilt conflicts, internal conflicts which are never ending. In India too we have seen new conflict zones emerging every decade since independence and none of these internal conflicts are anywhere close to an end. Mizoram has been the only exception. South Asia will continue to be a region of political and military turbulence, which will impact India also. The increase in employment of Army in internal conflicts cannot be ruled out in future. There is likely to be a temptation to employ Indian Army to counter Naxalites, on one pretext or the other. Slowly but steadily army will find itself totally committed to combat Naxalites!

Lt Gen (Retd) VK Nayar, PVSM, SM, in an article "Civil Military Relations", published in USI journal Oct–Dec 2008 writes "Indian Armed Forces like any other institution are conditioned by their functional imperative to meet the growing threats to the country. They have also been influenced by societal imperatives, that is why they are different from the Pakistan Army; in spite of common heritage and traditions of British Indian Army. There is an inherent and natural conflict between the two as military institutions which reflect only social values may be incapable of performing their military role effectively, while the military institutions shaped and influenced by military imperatives will be difficult to contain within the society. Interaction and balance between the two is the hub of civil- military relations." How true it is when it comes to routine and prolonged use of military power in dealing with internal security situations.

During initial years of my army career, I was posted in Nagaland along with my battalion in August 1964 with the primary task of combating insurgency. On completion of four decades of army service, I have retired and my son who is an army officer may have to combat insurgency in North East for at least another 20 years. We see no political solution. Can we draw a conclusion that Army did not use its military might to combat insurgency? Of course, it must be acknowledged, that while dealing with internal security situations army does not employ its total combat power. We are probably the only army in the world to have enforced on ourselves the concept and operational philosophy of use of minimum force while dealing with internal security situation. It has its own advantages and disadvantages. But in the long run the philosophy has paid us, though at a very high cost of casualties to our own officers and men. Insurgency in NE started from Nagaland and despite prolonged and sustained operations of army and other paramilitary forces it could not be eliminated. Of course, it has been contained and managed to so-called "manageable and acceptable level of violence" (as the politicians and bureaucrats ably advised by self appointed experts and analysts prefer to call it). Does it mean that the new role of the army (though not stated in writing) is to manage the conflict and violence and keep it at the minimal level? Instead of total elimination of insurgency in Nagaland, it spread to Manipur, Mizoram, Tripura, some parts of Arunachal Pradesh and Assam too. Some insurgent groups are now in the process of organizing themselves in Meghalay also. All this has happened due to political motives of the so-called local politicians and political parties, indifferent and ineffective governance of states which gave a rise and impetus to separatist tendencies, increase in violence, resulting in more and more troops, army units, paramilitary forces, raising of control headquarters and so on. It is not that Army is incapable of controlling insurgency but the vested interests, some political parties, some lower rank civil government functionaries, contractors, land, jungle, mining mafia, drug and weapon smugglers want the unrest to continue for their narrow political, monetary and other personal gains. Insurgency, in fact has become cottage industry in most of the states of north-east. Same holds good for Naxalites.

For wrong and narrow political policies and monitory gains in Punjab, law and order situation got out of control and became alarming resulting in large scale deployment of army for OPERATION BLUESTAR and thereafter to combat terrorism in the state. Initially, from the deployment of two infantry division size force the army deployment in Punjab increase many fold to combat terrorism. Finally, the people of Punjab brought an end to terrorism, though mistakenly the credit has been given to just a few people. It was the Indian Army and our brave Punjab Police duly supported and assisted by people of Punjab, which brought the violence to minimum level, whereas in other steps resolution of conflict could be initiated from the position of strength. The use of military power during initial stages of terrorism did help in restoration of normalcy in Punjab which has been been ensured by Punjab Police.

In J&K due to ineffective, incapable and unconcerned governance in the state, the terrorism gained in strength. The state administration was inefficient to the justified needs and aspirations of simple people of the Kashmir valley. The unhappiness, dissatisfaction, helplessness and frustration of the people of Kashmir was exploited by some local anti-national elements, few so-called politicians, supported by some elements of the state government functionaries. This was further exploited, encouraged, supported and sustained by Pakistan resulting in a situation of internal revolt. Not only Pakistan but also some countries from Middle East and even Europe helped the anti-national elements in creating adverse situation for Government of India which however continued to ignore the inputs and warnings given by army authorities about dangerous situation developing in Kashmir. When the situation got out of control again the panic button was pressed resulting in large scale deployment of army in Kashmir to combat the so-called terrorism, cross border terrorism, proxy war and low intensity conflict. In reality it was an insurgency which subsequently developed into terrorism. It needs to be considered that in India there is a tendency and temptation to club everything under law and order problem. The term insurgency means revolt, or rebellion which neither the state government nor the central government were willing to accept this fact. Once the situation goes beyond control, the tendency is to employ army/military power. From the induction of eight mountain divisions in Kashmir in the initial stages the the force level has increased many fold. New Division headquarters, Corp. headquarters, Rashtriya Rifle Force headquarters are the indicators though these were desirable. Their presence in J&K will be desirable due to peculiar threats from across the border. We should not give up to the demands made by few so called politicians from Kashmir Valley, to reduce force level. It is to the credit of Indian Army, duly supported by Paramilitary forces, state police, and most important of all people of Kashmir to have brought the violence to manageable level. Of course, navy and air force also made useful contribution. Despite great provocation, unacceptable losses to our troops, and junior officers the Indian Army once again enforced on itself the principle of use of minimum force while combating terrorism in Kashmir Valley. Nowhere in the world one comes across the operational philosophy of use of minimum force in dealing with internal security challenges. Indian Army must be given due credit for this. Even in Sri Lanka, during IPKF operations, Indian Army did not use its full combat power against LTTE, to avoid harm to innocent people as also collateral damage. Just compare the combat power used by Sri Lanka Armed Forces in combating LTTE, combat power used by the USA in Iraq, the USA and the NATO force in Afghanistan and now US Army and Pakistan Armed Forces in Western Pakistan to combat terrorism, Taliban and al-Qaeda. There is a temptation among some think tanks, specialists, experts and analysts who have never handled a single terrorist to suggest (sitting in air-conditioned and isolated environment, far, far away from theatre of operation) that Indian Army should adopt the same operational philosophy and use of maximum combat power in our fight against terrorists, insurgents, and to crush insurgency and terrorism the same way as has been done by USA in Iraq and USA, NATO as well as Pakistan in Afghanistan. This will be an utter foolishness,unacceptable in Indian context. Our self-appointed experts deliberately or otherwise fail to comprehend and accept that US and NATO forces are combating the terrorism on foreign soil where they have no concern for the loss of innocent lives and collateral damage due to use of military power. Would they use the military power the same way if they were to combat terrorist or terrorism within the geographical limits of their own country? We must accept the fact that Indian Army operates to respond to internal security challenges within India, among our own people, some of whom have been misguided, misled, misinformed and mismanaged. Therefore the Indian Army will continue to exercise restraint in using full combat power in dealing with internal security challenges. This will continue to be a biggest challenge to Indian Army.

Even the Naxalite problem which is our own creation due to misgovernance, has been fully exploited, used and abused by just a few political parties for their narrow and momentary political gains. Instead of being controlled and eliminated, Naxalite movement has now spread over 13 states and 153 districts of India. Again some self- styled experts have described the 'Red Corridor' running from Nepal (Himalays) to Indian Ocean or from Pashupati to Tirupati. Every state government has been claiming publicly that they have been able to control or manage the Naxalite violence, secretly sounding the Central Government to deploy army to combat Naxalites. Home Ministers of India, and even the Prime Minister is on record to state on several occasions and at several forums that the greatest threat to India's internal security is from Naxalites. The recent incident in West Bengal (Lalgarh) has clearly proved that the Maoist (Naxalite) threat in West Bengal is an indicator of the growing strength of violent left-wing groups and of the unwillingness of the state to confront them. With an estimated strength (committed cadre) of around 10,000 all over India, it is not beyond the power of the Central and state governments to defeat, disband, and rehabilitate them over the next couple of years. But through sheer callousness and carelessness, we have allowed a minor threat to grow into a "Frankenstein". One of the state governments seems to have worked out the quantum of troops, as to how many battalions, brigades, divisions, armed helicopters, special forces, UAVs will be needed to combat Naxalites in that particular state! It is to the credit of the ministry of home affairs, probably based on the advice of the ministry of defence and Army HQ, that the temptation to deploy Indian Army in combating Naxalites has been resisted so far, since it will be the most disastrous course of action. It is hoped that Indian Army does not get committed directly or indirectly in combating Naxalites in future, because the problem is the creation of respective state governments and only they can resolve it. There will be attempts to gradually involve the army under the pretext of incidental presence, training in Naxalite infested areas, keep a discrete eye, provide advice, and train the state police and paramilitary forces. This is exactly how army was deployed in Pubjab in 1990 to combat terrorism. The initial pretext was that of training and gradually army found itself totally committed in counter-terrorist operations.

When army is deployed too often and for long durations in internal security for management and control of violence to acceptable level (which is a new concept adopted by our governing mechanism since the last few years) it places very heavy and professionally unrealistic demands on soldiers, junior leaders and commanders specially up to the rank of colonels (commanding officers of the combat units deployed). The army is organized, equipped, trained and motivated to meet classical, conventional and external threats. The troops are trained and motivated to shoot to kill the external enemy. The combat philosophy is geared up to use maximum combat power to destroy the enemy and also total destruction and suppression of enemy's capabilities and will to offer any resistance during conventional war. We have seen the use of such force recently by USA in Iraq, Afghanistan and by Israel in Lebanon and Gaza strip. Internal security operations which could be termed as open ended with no time limits, run a risk of some civilian casualties and losses; collateral damages to civil property. This leads to wrong perceptions about army's high handedness which perception is totally wrong. This misperception is bound to lead to erosion of goodwill amongst the local population where the operations are conducted.

Many local political parties, politicians, the so-called NGOs (which are mostly funded from abroad, and some anti-national elements like Hurriat Conference in Kashmir, are always eager to accuse and malign Government of India and army by carefully manipulated and twisted projection of events. They misinform our young journalists (both print and electronic) by giving wrong inputs. One should never blame the media because it is responsible to the society. They will report what is told to them. There are many incidents of false propaganda against central government and army in Kashmir and North- East. Even reputed Channels like BBC have been culpable of misreporting of events in Kashmir. I have indisputable proof to prove my point. A dangerous feeling of "Us" and "They" is deliberately engendered by some local political interests. This adversely affects mindset and tolerance level of our young soldiers and junior leaders. When soldiers and young officers feel cheated and robbed of their clean image due to false allegations; there emerges a shadow of doubt in their mind and they start questioning (though they do not voice their views and feeling openly, through media which is a good practice) the very purpose and justification and also the usefulness of their prolonged deployment in internal security. Only those commanders who have commanded troops in sensitive areas under stressful conditions can realize these facts and harsh ground realities. The people who look up to the army for their security and protection from external threats— due to false propaganda at times— feel antagonized. Thus the army finds itself in catch 22 situation, wherein the efficient, courageous and exemplary performance of its role and duties is fraught with the risk of damaging reputation as has recently happened in Assam, Manipur and Kashmir.

Yet another challenges of prolonged deployment of army in internal security is how to avoid adverse impact on conventional preparedness. There is always a danger of "shift" in focus and priorities from classical conventional role of meeting external threats to the daily issues of internal security, since it becomes the immediate major concern of political leadership and bureaucracy. This also impacts the armed forces. Many experts may not agree with me, but this is a harsh truth and reality. One of the examples is the shift in the focus from the long term threats from China to combating terrorism in J&K. This shift in focus resulted in thinning out forces from eastern theatre to boost up the strength in J&K. I do not wish to name the formations which moved from eastern theatre to northern Sector. Have we ever considered the fact that we may be lured into complacency and forced to shift our focus from eastern theatre, and this may be a part of some long term well thought of grand design which can have very serious repercussions on our country's long term security interests, territorial integrity and stability? This issue needs a very serious and honest appraisal and analysis. Why do we ignore China's claim on Arunachal Pradesh? Are the Chinese non-serious and light-hearted to lay claim to Arunachal Pradesh?

Kargil episode is yet another example of the dangerous implications of shift in our focus. When our adversary finds us totally engrossed in "Internal Security", he will exploit the situation to its utmost advantage. This is what exactly happened in Kargil. While the focus of political leaders, governing mechanism, intelligence agencies and even security mechanism was on Siachen Glacier (number of highly publicized visits of powers that be and media coverage is an indicator) and terrorism in Kashmir Valley, nobody thought of Kargil sector. No wonder everyone was taken by surprise in Kargil. Despite of brave front put up by everyone to cover our own inadequacies the harsh fact cannot be ignored. It is to the credit of our brave soldiers, young officers, junior leaders and commanders up to the rank of colonel, that we retrieved Kargil from the hands of our adversary. We ignored the basic philosophy of governance that the weak have one weapon and that is the errors of those who think they are strong. Our adversary was fully aware of our weaknesses and totally exploited these. If we do not "wake up" now and handle the mechanism carefully we may be surprised again and again. Let us remember the statements of the foreign minister of Pakistan during Kargil war to BBC that there will be 10 more Kargils. Even General Musharraf repeatedly said while in power and afterwards that Kargil will continue to happen. Let us not make out too much of the "Kargil Report" prepared by some of our eminent experts. Kargil report is nothing but a cover up of our inadequacies and shift in our focus. No wonder the report is more voluminous than the Mahabharat and the Ramayana! It is the dangerous shift in our focus that prevented us from anticipating and analyzing as to what was going on in the minds of our adversary both internal and external. Despite all the technological advancements in today's world there is no device, technology, UAVs, and even satellites which can "read, analyse, and anticipate the mindset of our adversaries. It is hoped that the powers that be of today and future will not repeat the same mistakes again. Kargil will not happen at Kargil— Kargil like situation can take place any where else in India. The 26/11 at Mumbai is an example.

It is therefore necessary to understand the implications, limitations and consequences of prolonged employment and use of military power to meet Internal Security Challenges. Prolonged deployment can be counterproductive in the long run. After certain length of time and even increase in force levels in a conflict area the "Law of Diminishing Return" starts applying. Military operations and prolonged deployment of army is useful and effective only initially and to some extent.

If we sincerely want to avoid prolonged employment/ deployment of army in internal security management, all organs of our governing mechanism, political parties and leadership must send a clear message within India and across the borders, that:

Do not believe in the alliance of money and machine guns; because your children will not inherit the money, but they may end up holding machine guns and bombs which will destroy others and also the children holding the guns.

Internal Security threats, insurgencies, terrorism do not disappear suddenly. Unless a long-drawn process of elimination of root causes is ensured, internal threats will resurface in one form or the other. There are limitations of use and usefulness of military power to meet the challenges of internal security.

The author has very rich experience of combating insurgency and terrorism. He has served in North- East, Punjab, and Kashmir— All of which are terrorism afflicted. He served at Counter-Insurgency and Jungle Warfare School. He served as deputy director and additional director general of Military Operations at Army HQ and also as additional director general of perspective planning at Army HQ.

Chapter 6

Future Warfare

*Maj Gen Anjan Mukherjee**

> War is nothing but a duel on a large scale.
>
> —*Carl Von Clausewitz**

Warfare is an eternal institution of nature. Its motives may vary but fall into the trinity of dominance, violence and honour. While there is no recorded history of when wars commenced, it is as old as human civilization itself. History reveals that major conflicts took place during the agrarian revolution around 6000 BC and continued in some form or other thereafter. In contemporary times, it has survived the industrial revolutions of the nineteenth century and industrial scientific revolution of the twentieth century. Growth of civilization and human

*The writer is presently with National Defence College, New Delhi.

intelligence saw wars and conflict growing in its reach and dimensions adapting itself to the changes in cultural, social, political, economical and technological structure of the times. History is replete with instances of changing object of waging a war or joining a conflict, sometimes at strategic level and during other times at lesser threshold. War or threat of war, therefore, has the unique power to reach decisions or get international interventions during present times. It is also a projection of comprehensive national power of a nation.

War and warfare has the unique ability to change local, regional and world politics, national alignments and national honour. War may not ensure national security goals of a nation but defeat certainly guarantees its failure. Influence of international conflicts and politics has substantial influence in a nation's domestic safety and security. Involvement of USSR in Afghanistan and in consequence of the US involvement, dismantling of USSR as a nation and rise of Taliban, al-Qaeda and international terrorism of a kind never seen before, along with consequent threat and security issues are representations of evolving nature of future wars.

Dimensions of Future Wars

Future wars will be shaped by a range of post-modern changes in politics, culture and society as well as asymmetries of human `Will`, Organization, national patience and unresolved issues between nation states as also non-state actors. Asymmetries of national 'Will' are related to a nation's survival or stake of vital national interests. Asymmetry of this nature played a role in conflicts in Vietnam, Somalia, and Iraq, and now in Afghanistan. An asymmetry of 'Will' leads the antagonist with the higher stake to be willing to bear greater costs, accept greater risks and undertake actions, which the less committed antagonist might eschew on moral or legal grounds. Asymmetries of 'Will' are most relevant at the level of 'Grand Strategy`. Napoleon once said, "In war the morale is to the material as three to one." Future wars will involve different ethical and legal standards and may involve weapons of mass destruction and space based warfare. In the contemporary security environment short term benefits through terrorism, ethnic cleansing etc may gain prominence, as they highlight 'Asymmetry of Will' of a culture and social structure. However, its long term benefits to antagonists are not proved by history. Hitler's failure towards ethnic cleansing of Jews, terrorism as an art of warfare adopted by LTTE, all have fallen to their doom.

'Asymmetries of Patience' of a set of individuals namely al-Qaeda leadership or nations namely the USA in case of Iraq, have given rise to high intensity warfare and induction of high technology for destruction and human succour. 'Asymmetries of Patience' have a cultural component as well. While nation states prefer quick resolution of armed conflict due to a sense on part of its leaders that the public support for any use of force that does not involve vital national interest has a limited life span. Furthermore, economies too have substantial influence in warfare. Western nations are, therefore, largely instinctively impatient seeking quick resolution of international military problems. Uneasiness of longer stay in Iraq and Afghanistan is well documented in the United States. In stark contrast, Asian perspective is one with greater patience and willingness to prevail in a conflict that may last for years or decades. Economic and political strength of Asian nations may define this asymmetry of patience between western and Asian culture.

'Asymmetries of Organization' have left its footprints in the evolution of warfare. Organizational strengths of a nation or a warring state or non-state actors have many a time dictated commencement and intensity of war. Smaller groups like al-Qaeda, Taliban, LTTE and other terrorist groups have been able to take on the might of a nation or a group of nations due to their networked organization. Future wars may also witness its manifestation in various forms.

'Asymmetry of Technology' and effect of revolution of military affairs have defined future of warfare in the past. In conflicts where the lesser technologically strong antagonist does not have the ability to confront the opponent who is advanced in technology, he may counter it by asymmetries in warfare namely terrorism, insurgency, suicide-bombing, kidnapping, maritime piracy, dirty nuclear bombs, increasing the threat to non-military personnel in a target country and thus protracting the war. Consequent effect on the state of finances and national morale is expected to be substantial. Such actions will lead to substantial media exposure thus achieving one of the aims of the lesser antagonist. It may also influence more people to join them and thus expand its organization and influence; thereby increasing the reach of such conflict.

Paradigms of Future Conflict

Transition of conflict and war from traditional conventional war became more pronounced once the Cold War ended. Many theories related to continuation of concepts of conventional war as part of long term conflict between two warring nation states with terrorism as a short term dimension of conflict, became prominent. Robert Kaplan's *Anarchy Theory*, Michael Brown's *Rationale of Internal Conflict Theory*, *Wave Theory* of Warfare propounded by Avin and Heidi Toffler, Paul Collier's *Greed versus Grievance Theory* and Samuel P Huntington's '*Clash of Civilization*' have underlined the various causes, conduct and character of future conflicts and wars. Greed, erosion of state authority, ethnicity, demographic fissures, hostility between nations over culture and religion will act as an impelling force in generating violence and conflict. Various kinds of wars that may be fought in future between nations will follow well-defined sequence as a part of state stratagems and as a function of overall grand strategy. Thus, a modern conventional war of future will also represent a multi-concerned, multi-spectral asymmetrical conflict.

A newer form of asymmetrical conflict waged by a state, state sponsored non-state actors or a group many graduate from public disobediences to move up the escalatory ladder to dissension and then demand of autonomy, statehood and independence; examples of which are found in Pakistan and Kashmir.

Future Wars will therefore, be fought in a globalized environment. It would range from propaganda wars namely the Iraq war, psychological war undermining the morale of the enemy, economic war through trade embargo and economic sanctions; diplomatic war, demographic war, terrorism and insurgency; space based wars, nuclear, biological and chemical wars and conventional wars with one or all of the elements included in its spectrum of application.

Future Military and Non-Military Wars

Chinese writers Qiao Liang and Wang Xiangsui's in their work entitled, 'Unrestricted Warfare', published in February 1999 have highlighted the primary fact that even in a post modern world, warfare has not been banished but has only assumed more complex extensions and concealed and subtle forms. Therefore, military means alone will be inadequate to contest these multi-dimensional threats arising out of economic, cultural, political, ethnic, demographic and religious issues. The principles of war of the 21st century would be no longer about using armed forces to compel an enemy to submit to ones will but rather about using all means including armed forces and non-armed forces, military and non-military, lethal and non-lethal, to compel the enemy to accept ones interests. Future wars will transcend all boundaries and limits, if international structures do not intervene and defuse the issues leading to conflicts.

Future wars are unlikely to remain in single domain. With the advent of internet, Ethernet, and fiction level technologies, future wars are likely to be combination of one or more in the military-non-military domains of warfare. A newer supra domain combinations or grouping of battlefields will emerge for future warfare. Concept of Beyond Limits, combined wars extending to the realms of Omni directionally, synchrony, limited objectives-unlimited measures, asymmetry, and multi directional coordination with asymmetry warfare at the core of unrestricted warfare will gain ground. Such wars will aim to achieve enhancement of own power and evolve situational interests for future wars.

Future Wars: Road Ahead

The twenty first century is likely to observe more of internal instability related insurgencies and terrorism. Security forces of nations will be confronting internal enemies like separatists, militias, insurgents, terrorists, armed criminal cartels, drug mafia. Protracted, complex, ambiguous armed conflicts rather than short politically and ethically clear ones leading to decisive outcomes would dominate it. These and other political, economic and regional issues between many belligerents will define the future wars. The issue arises as to what is the future of conventional battles and wars since the present world security order has shown that the nations are constrained from overt military aggression due to globalization, economical constraints and evolvement of international structures. The armed forces of all nations are likely to be involved in promoting internal stability and confronting internal enemies, whether separatists, militias, insurgents, terrorists, armed criminal cartels, or something similar. The international efforts towards containing terror will dominate the first two decades of the 21st century. Yet evolving international equations and national security interests of nations, evolution of military tools for fourth generation warfare will ensure that the threat of a nation's reputation, honour, independence, sovereignty and its stake in the comity of nations will grossly depend upon its conventional and strategic military power. It will also reflect in its Gross National Power.

Future wars are likely to use all available networks—political, economic, social and military—to convince the enemy's political decision makers that their strategic goals are either unachievable or too costly for the perceived benefit.

Rooted in the fundamental precept that superior political 'Will' when properly employed can defeat greater economic and military power, future wars will make use of society's network to carry on its fight. Unlike previous generations of warfare it may not result in overt defeat of enemy's military forces, instead via the networks, it will directly attack the strategically operational cohesion of enemy decision makers to destroy the enemy's 'Will'. Future wars will see limits of high technology warfare and necessity of boots on ground. The profession of arms will become bigger, larger and more lethal to modernize the armed forces throughout the world. Common assumption that military trained for major combat operations would be able to easily handle less violent operations like peace keeping and counter insurgency having been proved mostly wrong, future armed forces will need specialized counter-insurgency forces. Future wars, therefore, are likely to be lengthy and a mix of asymmetrical and conventional warfare. While initial two decades of the twenty first century may confront more of asymmetrical warfare, conventional warfare threat will continue and possibly, enhance in view of likely change in the world order, clash of interests of national and non-state actors, clash of culture and religions. In this scenario, it is not possible to rule out the use of weapons of mass destructions during the future wars.

Asymmetry is a future of all warfare, albeit a more prominent feature in some cases than others are. As noted already, terrorism, which pits small numbers of typically fanatical people against the regular might of states, is just the extreme example of asymmetrical conflict. However, regular and irregular warfare frequently are fused. We must be wary of the tyranny of categories. It is convenient to analyze regular warfare between states separately from irregular warfare between non-state bodies and states, but it is essential to remember that the distinction may mislead.

The ignoble al-Qaeda is not a state. Neither does it exist beyond political and physical geography, nor is it ignorable. The distinctly regular military operations can coerce the countries that support, or even tolerate, terrorist activity on their soil. In principle, at least, this strategic fact explains the fate of Taliban Afghanistan. The asymmetrical dimension to all warfare is about the competitive endeavour to exploit one's strengths and offset one's weaknesses, against enemies whose strengths and weaknesses will be distinctive.

Chapter 7

Human Resource Management in the Indian Army

*Lt Gen Mukesh Sabharwal, AVSM**, VSM*

"Human resource development is an essential command function and, in this context, it needs to be understood that the soldier of tomorrow has to be an innovator who can combine imagination and knowledge with action."[1]

–Indian Army Doctrine

The Indian Army in the present day diverse socio-economic environment is undergoing a transformation in the field of equipment, strategy and tactics which has a positive impact on the performance of the soldier. As the nation marches towards prosperity, the need of the hour is to consolidate the army into a highly motivated, optimally equipped and modernized,

---

*The writer is presently Adjutant General in Indian Army.

operationally ready force, capable of functioning in a joint services environment across the spectrum of conflict[2].

Human resources development needs continuous attention even as the transformation is taking place. This assumes importance as the strength of Indian Army has always been its soldier. It is apt to say that institutions do not transform—people do; platforms and organizations do not defend the country—people do; and units and formations do not sacrifice and take risks for the Nation—people do. Thus, without highly skilled, competent and dedicated people, it does not matter how lethal our weapons are or how strategically responsive our formations grow; soldiers are the most important enablers of our strategy. This is a well-recognized fact in the Indian Army Doctrine 2004, wherein speaking of ushering in a Revolution in Military Affairs (RMA), the document states "While doing so, aspects relating to orchestration of human resources and re-orientation of training, which are imperative for unleashing the full potential of emerging technologies, must be factored in as technology alone cannot influence the course of war unless there is a transformation in the manner defence forces think, train and fight"[3].

The human resource management challenge that the army faces is far more than any multinational company. Sheer numbers make it so. There are several similarities when compared to any commercial organization. These are hierarchies and functions, leaders and followers, teams, meetings and strategy sessions, very high emphasis on 'delivering the goods' and above all, a sense of organizational social responsibility that makes it our most reliable asset during times of crisis. Perhaps the one big difference between the defence forces and commercial corporations is the raison d'être. The objective of the defence forces is to lend the nation the ability to "speak softly, but carry a big stick"[4] or to maintain its sovereignty and its ability to act in its own national interest; instead of profit-orientation, which is the objective in commercial corporations. The attitude is to do 'whatever-it-takes', for there can be no price too high for the stakes for which the military exists.

Managing Human Resources

In the Indian Army, the adjutant general's branch executes the functions related to human resource management. The mission of the branch through human resource management is to assist the Indian Army to meet its strategic and national security goals by attracting, maintaining and managing its soldiers effectively. The operative word is "fit" i.e. ensure a fit between the management of soldiers, and the overall strategic direction of the Indian Army. Human resource management encompasses a wide variety of subjects. The attempt here is to focus on the key areas.

Macro level activities include manpower planning, raising and re-organization of headquarters, formations and units in consultation with the operational staff besides induction into the service i.e. selection, recruitment and commissioning.

The AG's Branch formulates and reviews terms and conditions of service, including pay and allowances as well as pension and terminal benefits; lays down policies regarding documentation and control of records including policies pertaining to civilian employees in the army and Gorkha personnel.

The Branch is also responsible for in-service discipline and vigilance issues related to all personnel and all legal matters concerning the army. Ceremonial and welfare aspects including grant of honours, awards and maintenance of morale is part of its duty as is ensuring the good health of all ranks. Ex-servicemen's welfare is also an important function.

Challenges

The basic premise of human resource management is that humans are not machines and varieties of activities highlight this human face of the Indian Army. A vibrant economy, globalization, advanced technology, a deluge of data and information, and a flourishing private sector, all offer innumerable opportunities to India in the 21st century. This profound change fundamentally alters the traditional, social and cultural values of any society irrevocably. All round development means moving rapidly to a society of knowledge workers i.e. in our case from a 'brawn force' to a "balanced brain cum brawn force". With all organizations vying for the best, talent will be at a premium, attracting, retaining and motivating the best. This will remain a constant challenge for the army. Having people-oriented and transparent policies, selection system, training and development, appraisal, leadership styles and organizational climate will help meet the challenge.

These changes have also affected the Indian defence forces in many ways. On one hand, it is assisting in the modernization of the forces and on the other hand, the lure of lucre has created complex challenges for our volunteer defence forces, as the society connects with the men in uniform. The present values and standards of the defence forces are not abstract concepts whose genesis lies solely in the demands of battle. In fact, they are the very foundations of the services whereon reposes the entire. They reflect our rich history and evolution over the years into what we are today, a formidable army with a human face.

The credo of the Indian Military Academy, Dehra Dun, "The safety, honour and welfare of your country come first, always and every time. The honour, welfare and comfort of the men you command come next. Your own ease, comfort and safety come last, always and every time"[5] is an apt and unchanging description of our core values. These values are absolute and non-negotiable, irrespective of any societal changes, now or in the future. Though this may be explained as natural bonding which is inevitably formed due to serving together under difficult conditions, it is only an unflinching faith in one's duty and the supreme consideration to uphold the 'Izzat' of the Regiment which enable soldiers to volunteer for risky missions or at times to show restraint, even when doing so involves personal danger. Integrity and honesty are another set of values, which are vital for success in any battle, as no scope for deviation exists when the life of men depends upon honest and resolute decisions by the leaders.

Changed circumstances

Nuclear families are now the norm rather than the exception. In the rural areas, the land holdings are progressively whittling down. This has resulted in an increased number of small families who are devoid of the traditional support system from the extended or joint family. However, practical difficulties due to exigencies of service have rendered it difficult for men in uniform to strike a reasonable balance between his home and professional front. This highlights the importance of basic amenities like housing, education and medical cover. While these aspirations are somewhat subdued among youth from rural and semi-urban areas, they are commonplace in the case of those from bigger cities. The requirements of the army are to envisage accommodating the aspirations within the defined structures of the defence forces without compromising on our organizational terms of reference. The endeavour thus, is to attract the best talent and retain organizational efficiency, in spite of the sweeping changes.

The rapid changes in society and the aspirations of the youth bring us to the underlying necessity to embrace changed circumstances. The defence forces of the country have themselves undergone many successful transitions by embracing new circumstances. Independence in 1947 brought one such massive change, rapid modernization and expansion, post 1962 war was another transition, which perhaps culminated in a brilliant campaign severing East Pakistan. In the recent years, the prowess acquired in fighting successful counter-insurgency operations by an essentially conventional army may be termed as a successful adaptation. Thus, considerable flexibility exists in the organization and our solutions can be tailored 'in-house', using in-house experience and expertise already available within the army. However, even as we can justly pride ourselves in being a truly professional army, with enormous fighting potential, there are certain realities, which we have to face.

Early Retirement: Given its harsh working conditions and its role, the army must necessarily maintain a youthful profile. Thus, a Jawan recruited at 18-year of age could retire when he is just 37-year old. He thus does not get the benefit of earning a salary, and consequent increments until the age of 60 years. Given his limited educational qualifications thus far and an all too frequent desire not to leave his village, second career opportunities for the soldier have been less than adequate. There is no real pecuniary compensation for this rather serious handicap faced by most soldiers. This is possibly one of the reasons for a low life expectancy.

Life Expectancy: The life expectancy of an Indian Army soldier in general is less than the national life expectancy of 64.7 years approximately. This is probably a consequence of a combination of harsh working environment where the army operates in difficult conditions, lack of adequate education, early retirement and conditions of health and hygiene in villages, where most of our veterans live post retirement.

Increasing Complexities of Battlefield and Second Career: Increasing complexities of the battlefield demand greater cerebral involvement. The army has been extremely mentally mobile in this regard, and has tailored its training, accordingly. The requirement then is to translate this enhancement in cerebral standards into educational qualifications, thereby facilitating the second career for our Jawans, without compromising on operational readiness and effectiveness.

A Weakening Family Support System: The number of Jawans whose families continue to live in joint families is continually reducing. With this, there is a requirement of constantly addressing newer issues like a soldiers aspirations for his children, greater requirement of married and separated family accommodation besides security for separated families, addressing issues like marital discord and a host of other complex issues.

The Way Ahead: The defence forces already have a time-tested orientation towards managing human resources, which need a review besides addressing the genuine aspirations and needs of the soldiers.

The need is to aim for a high quality intake, which can rapidly adapt to the advances in modern technology and meet the demands of the future battlefield. We should also start early and catch men young to absorb the right talent. Better management of the media and encouragement to organizations like National Cadet Corps and Bharat Scouts and Guides would help project the image of the Indian Army better among the youth of the nation. The positive impact of popular cinema, like in the case of "Border" or "Lakshya" on the psyche of an average youth will go a long way in conveying a positive image to the target population. A younger age profile of the leadership will provide the "cutting edge" to the army. This is possible by effective cadre management to include reducing shortage of officers by changing officer-manning ratio between regular and support cadres and the opening up of an additional Officers Training Academy, if necessary.

To motivate and have a robust force capable of operating across the spectrum of conflict, there is an impending need to provide top class healthcare not only at the bigger stations but also at certain satellite stations, which are reachable from rural areas. There is need to establish state-of-the-art hospitals at each Command on the line of the Research and Referral Hospital. The Indian Army in the present day environment is engaged in counter-insurgency and counter-terrorism wherein the requirement is immediate medical treatment at dispersed locations and speedy and timely evacuation by land or air.

For development of a motivated force, the focus of the soldiers has to be on the assigned task. Personnel need to maintain high military standards, their quality of life should be commensurate with the sacrifices the nation expects them to make and the family support system for the soldier has to be top of the line so that he does not have to look over his shoulder or worry for folks back home. To compensate for the deprivation there is a constant need to review the terms and conditions of service related to promotion prospects, in service pay and allowances and pension, as to provision of high quality and affordable necessities like housing, education and medical facilities, including wards and next of kin. The partial implementation of Ajai Vikram Singh Committee report has addressed the aspirations of officers to some extent. The proposal with regard to 'Peel Factors' of this report will help sustain the same. Similarly, they have taken some steps for an assured career.

The progression in respect of men needs further attention, especially in view of short career spans when compared to their civilian counterparts. There is also a need to ensure that a watertight legal framework is in place to enable soldiers to operate effectively in counter-insurgency/counter-terrorism related actions, and to honour martyrs and brave hearts not only by gallantry awards but monetary benefits and jobs to the next of kin and most importantly by " Izzat".

The army goes an extra mile to ensure that all soldiers remain impervious to extraneous considerations. While the acceptance by the government of recommendations of the Sixth Pay Commission is a welcome step, there are limitations in terms of pay and allowances, which are not able to keep pace with opportunities in the private sector. The shoring up intangible means can minimize the impact i.e. by creating healthy working relationships between superiors and subordinates, a positive, understating and helping attitude, transparency in dealings and delegation of responsibilities to the appropriate levels. However, there is a need for addressing the requirement of catering for the lost years of earning between early retirement and 60 years, which are available to the soldier's civilian counterparts to earn increment and salary, resulting also in higher pensions and longer life spans. The separate Seventh Pay Commission announced for the defence forces will examine this issue.

In keeping with reality, the army deals with the offences involving moral turpitude more harshly even as they are loosening the strict hierarchical structures. The government has recognized the requirement of establishing an effective grievance redressal mechanism, the absence of which has forced an increased number of service personnel to civil courts in the past. The recent institution of the Armed Forces Tribunal is a step in the right direction, as this will lead to availability of prompt and sound legal remedy at a minimum cost, even as offering a forum for appeal for personnel aggrieved by military justice imparted to them.[6]

Welfare Measures

The army has started an ambitious Married Accommodation Project, which will considerably increase the satisfaction level in term of housing facilities. The need to increase the percentage of married accommodation authorized to units coming to peace locations for giving each married soldier opportunity to live with his family at least for a year or two is another important mental and physical booster. In addition, the Army Welfare Housing Organization (AWHO) has carved a niche for itself by providing quality housing at an affordable cost.

The Army Group Insurance Fund is a pioneer in providing insurance cover and inexpensive loans. Besides, the army is providing varied educational opportunities to army personnel and their families. This has made significant contribution in meeting the aspirations of our officers and men. Army Group Insurance Fund has helped lend security to our excellent soldiers and their families and has improved their lives.

The Army Welfare Education Society has grown into an organization providing enormous varieties of educational opportunities to the dependants of our soldiers. In fact, there is a requirement to expand the educational facilities at all major stations, particularly in terms of good residential schools.[7]

The Ex-servicemen Contributory Health Scheme is beginning to make a mark for itself by providing quality medical care to ex-servicemen. The 'in-house' examples of these professional organizations are worth emulating in other welfare related fields to meet the rising aspirations. Establishments of such autonomous bodies in other arenas like transit facilities and resettlement mechanism would also bear examination.

Second Career Option: The defence forces are essentially a hierarchical structure, where merit is predominant. This is an organizational requirement and there cannot be a mass proliferation of senior ranks. Thus, there is a need to absorb its personnel at the middle level into paramilitary forces, public sector undertakings and the private sector to offer post retirement and second career options, enable a longer working life, reduced pension bills and improve post retirement financial status of our soldiers. This permanent absorption will be a symbiotic relationship as these organizations shall benefit from the varied experience and ingrained values of these ex-servicemen who are still within the working age and retain considerable enthusiasm. Besides, from a national HR perspective, the need is to address this empirical problem of low life expectancy. The most obvious answer, with least damage to the exchequer, is to cater for a second career for the soldiers, enabling them to serve until his civilian counterparts, and reducing the pension bill. As of now, the exposure of army personnel to requisite orientation and management courses before they hang their uniform to begin another career. Today, veterans are in considerable demand even in the corporate, industrial and services sector, as corporate India has now woken up to the inherent strengths including high training standards, uncompromising ethics and loyalty of defence personnel; qualities which are treasured in any organization. Thus, the recent tie-up with reputed management institutes for pre-release courses and award of graduation degree to soldiers through Indira Gandhi National Open University (IGNOU). IGNOU is using the community college concept, recognizing in-service education and training activities undergone by soldiers as 'GYAN DEEP'. This meets the twin objectives of empowering soldiers educationally and providing an opportunity for a second career option. Further, this project will give a fillip to increase educational standards in the army.

Conclusion

The army is a microcosm of Indian society, from which it is drawn. A vibrant India has begun its march towards economic prosperity and the associated socio-economic changes have posed unique challenges to the defence forces. These can turn into an opportunity by effective management of change through refinements to selection and in-service management, meeting individual and financial aspirations of soldiers and through an autonomous redress mechanism. This will enhance the job satisfaction at all levels. Men have adequate time to enhance their educational and professional skills and look after their families. The overall aim of all these proposed changes is to ensure that we focus our efforts on the 'man behind the gun' and there is a continued strengthening of his moral fibre and the technical skills.

Accessibility and responsiveness by way of interactive websites and improved help lines is a positive step, already initiated in the right direction. The need of the hour is to be able to foresee the future, to analyze impending changes and introspection based on periodic feedback. The Indian Army endeavours to manage fair, just and expeditious dispensation of not only justice but also entitlements to all effectively through foresight, planning, organizing, leading and increasing functional efficiency. Needless to emphasize that weapons alone do not ensure victory, but it is the man behind the weapons who brings victory. Thus, the fighting machine—the soldiers— needs holistic care. In this lies the good of the army and the nation.

Endnotes

1. Indian Army Doctrine 2004, Chapter 6, Logistics, Section 20, Para 7.15.
2. General Deepak Kapoor, COAS, Indian Army, *The Sunday Indian*, 17/ 08/ 2008;

   http://www.thesundayindian.com/17082008/storyd.asp?sid=5371&pageno=1.
3. Indian Army Doctrine 2004, Part 1, Chapter 3 Operational Perspectives, Section 10, Para 3.39.
4. "Theodore Roosevelt, A Life", page 337; Nathan Miller; http://www.theodoreroosevelt.org/life/quotes.htm.
5. Sword of the Raj : the British army in India, 1747-1947; Roger Beaumont (1977), page xvii; Quoting a speech by Sir Philip Chetwode, C-in-C India, on the Opening of the IMA.
6. Ministry of Defence Annual Report 2009, page 16.
7. http://www.awes.nic.in.

Chapter 8

Keep the Armed Forces Apolitical

General VP Malik,
*PVSM, AVSM**

The tenth anniversary celebration of India's victory in Kargil war at Dras was a soul stirring spectacle. With the magnificent Tiger Hill and other mountain tops in the background, it was an emotional but a very dignified event. In the evening, candles were lit with great reverence to pay homage to the martyrs and the battleground on the mountain tops was lit up with mashals which was probably seen by Pakistan Army across the LoC (Line of Control). We remembered the sacrifices of our soldiers, the ferocity of the war, and the gallantry of the 'bravest of the brave'. Everyone present there felt immense national pride and fulfilment.

---

*The writer is a former Chief of the Army Staff, Indian Army.

I had yet another satisfaction that day. By laying a wreath to honour the Kargil martyrs at the India Gate Memorial, and lauding the armed forces for their sacrifice, valour and victory, Prime Minister Manmohan Singh had depoliticized the war.

India stands out as an example of democratic values where the armed forces are not involved in the affairs of the state. The Indian Army, Navy and Air Force inherited a legacy of being apolitical. Unlike many of our neighbouring countries, they have steadfastly preserved that legacy through the years. They have stuck to the concept of loyalty to the constitutionally elected government and thus enabled the nation to develop its unique democratic political ambience. Their oath is to the Constitution of India. Ideologies of political parties, whether in power or in the opposition, do not concern them. Needless to say, such an apolitical nature is a matter of great pride for the nation in general and for members of the armed forces in particular.

There are several reasons why the Indian military has remained apolitical over the years. The credit goes not only to the military and its traditions, but also to the political leadership, our egalitarian society and other well-established democratic institutions. Another important reason has been that, in the past, the political leaders or their party members did not make any serious attempt to politicize the armed forces. While some central and state services in India over the years are getting more and more politically influenced, the armed forces are among the last bastions to have escaped this trend. It is best that such a state of affairs continues.

This article is out of my concern that the democratic values and systems, which have kept the armed forces apolitical, do not get eroded. If we wish to see the men and women in uniform remain apolitical, the nation will need to be vigilant. It should help them to maintain such a tradition. Without political consensus on serious security issues affecting the country including internal security, there is a danger of the armed forces being politicized.

We fought the Kargil war at a time when our political system had been (and still is) going through the adjustments and compromises required by political coalitions, which are often more convenient and less principled. There was an interim government of the National Democratic Alliance (NDA). Mandatory general elections were due in early September 1999, or earlier. During and immediately after the war, despite emotional bonding of the nation and good wishes of the people at large, the armed forces were affected by political crossfire of a kind that had never been experienced in the past. On several occasions, the political parties that formed the government as well as the opposition managed to drag the armed forces into needless and unsavoury controversies that could adversely affect military systems, morale and their efficiency, and also harm their apolitical image and stature. The political exploitation of the Kargil war for electoral gains had many of us worried as it could undermine the neutral character of the armed forces and, in the process, affect its professionalism.

At the beginning of the war, political parties, like the rest of the nation, were unclear about the nature and size of the Pakistani infiltration, not to mention its purpose and rationale. When the fog of war enveloped the environment, and also when this fog started lifting, there was a justifiable concern in different quarters about the security situation in Kargil. Political parties in the opposition found an opportunity to hold the government responsible for political, intelligence and surveillance 'negligence'. This step, again, was justified, as a part of healthy national democratic process. But soon after that, some instances occurred wherein the army was unnecessarily involved in political controversies. One day, when I was out of station, the defence minister ordered a military team to brief the ruling party in the Parliament House. The opposition parties and the media created a justifiable furore when they learnt about it. On another occasion, the ruling party put up posters of the three chiefs in a political rally in Haryana.

The Opposition parties were not far behind. They held the government responsible for political, intelligence and surveillance negligence but also went out of their way to provide political support to a Brigadier who had been sidestepped (later dismissed from service) for ineffective command and control of the Kargil sector; something that had never happened during the course of any war before. When hostilities are on, commanders and staff officers who cannot deliver are often removed from their assignment. There are numerous such instances in our military history, especially during the 1962, 1965 and 1971 wars. In this instance, it was the army leadership and not the government that was involved in the decision. But some parties chose to exploit the episode for political reasons and thus encouraged him in his unlawful activities, even though such a move involved the army directly and tended to adversely affect the image of its leadership and the morale of the troops.

As the final outcome of the conflict started becoming clearer and the elections drew closer, Kargil became a political football. Everything to do with the Kargil conflict became an issue for election campaigns. There was an attempt either to put the armed forces on a pedestal or to pull them down from it. We had a hard time in keeping the political parties at bay: those blatantly cashing in on the Kargil victory and those attempting to neutralize this effect by castigating the ruling alliance. Several political leaders, with photo journalists in tow, motivated more by political factors than by a genuine concern for the wounded soldiers, made a beeline to the military hospitals to be photographed by their bedside while handing over gifts to them. Some organizations with well-recognized political agenda distributed copies of the Gita and Ramayana to the injured soldiers. Others wanted to distribute refrigerators and gift items, but only in the full glare of the media. When the Army PRO tried to stop visitors from taking media persons into the hospitals, both groups got visibly upset. The military leadership was accused of being politically partisan.

In August 1999, a large band of Vishwa Hindu Parishad (VHP) representatives descended upon South Block. They were carrying thousands of rakhis, apart from party and religious symbols, for the troops defending the Kargil border. They had brought along half-a-dozen photographers and insisted on meeting the Army chief (me). When they were refused permission, they forced their way into the Media Cell offices and handed over the rakhis to the staff, making sure that the TV cameras caught all the action. From the next day onwards, entry into the Army Headquarters part of the South Block was further restricted. The Army PRO soon sent out a notice to the effect that it was logistically not possible for the rakhis to be sent to the soldiers on the front.

No war in the past had influenced the domestic electoral dynamics in the way the Kargil crisis did. Inability of the political establishment to reach a national consensus at the time of war tended to affect the chain of military command and morale of the troops. We were anguished because we were getting sucked into electoral politics as a result of the blatant attempts to politicize the war for electoral advantage. In desperation, I had to send across a strong message through the media "Leave us alone: we are apolitical."

I brought all these happenings to Prime Minister Vajpayee's notice. He graciously acknowledged the wrong doings of his party workers, but his advice to me was: 'Do not be extrasensitive' I also met Dr Manmohan Singh, then the leader of the opposition in the Rajya Sabha. He was very courteous and appreciated the adverse consequences of the armed forces getting caught in political crossfire. He advised me to request the prime minister to call an all-party meeting on this matter. I did so. But like so many other issues in the government that are discussed and action promised, this matter too remained unattended.

Unfortunately, the attempts to make political capital out of sensitive issues pertaining to the armed forces did not stop even after the war or the elections. For some time, very few leaders from the opposition were seen at the military investiture ceremonies in the Rashtrapati Bhavan. Many senior serving and retired officers wondered why it should be so. We wondered how the political parties had conducted themselves after the India-China war in 1962. In this case, despite being placed in an adverse situation, the armed forces had successfully achieved the political mission and mandate given to them.

Even the Kargil victory day got politicized. Initially, the NDA Government celebrated it with great fervour. But after the election euphoria subsided, the government set the trend of quiet functions to 'avoid harming Indo-Pakistan relations'. This was a surprising stand, particularly when our senior political leaders seldom hesitate to meet and greet other world leaders and join victory celebrations commemorating the Second World War in different countries.

It must be remembered that the strategic environment of a nation keeps shifting but its history cannot be altered. Neglect of the military history of the nation reflects a weak strategic culture and a lack of military confidence. The opposition, in any case, shunned the 'Kargil victory' or its celebration.

In mid 2004, an attempt was made by some media persons to blame the past NDA Government for the delay in the use of air power during the Kargil war. This 'blame game' soon snowballed into a major controversy, leading to acrimonious political rivalry. Such a controversy could easily affect the joint working between the army and the air force. It goes to the credit of the then defence minister Pranab Mukherjee that, after taking into account the details of decisions taken in the thick of the Kargil war, he unequivocally set to rest all unwanted speculation, rising above narrow political interests.

In any other country, during the course of any war or after that, the armed forces are glorified, greatly respected and even treated with awe. In our country, very soon after the war, they feel forgotten and neglected by the political leadership. Why? This does not happen in other developed countries and democratic societies.

The point which I wish to emphasize is that the armed forces represent the most significant and ultimate instrument for sustaining the Indian polity. They are a manifestation of the collective political will of the Indian state. A soldier fights for the nation regardless of which party or group of parties is in power.

Even 10 years after the war, a Member of Parliament, Rashid Alvi had revived the old political controversy over the war by calling it a 'NDA show' with which the UPA had nothing to do. It needs to be stated here that the tenth anniversary victory celebration at Dras this year was primarily a Northern Command affair. There were no central leaders at the function to meet the martyrs' families or those who had participated in the war. Nor were they to remember the martyrs at India Gate on that day. It was under the media and public pressure that the Prime Minister took the initiative to visit India Gate memorial and lay the wreath. But as stated earlier, by this one action, hopefully, he has been able to depoliticize the Kargil war.

Now that this war stands depoliticized, my message to all young Members of Parliament across the political spectrum is to visit Siachen, Kargil and Dras and appreciate what their armed forces are capable of. And to our Member of Parliament Rashid Alvi, if he continues to harbour the old mindset, I wish to recall what late Lt Manoj Pandey, Param Vir Chakra winner in Kargil war, wrote in his very last letter, reflecting the national spirit of an India soldier, "I don't know what will happen at the next moment. But I can assure you and all countrymen that certainly we will push back the intruders at whatever cost".

Chapter 9

Indian Navy: Mission for Tomorrow

Admiral Nirmal Verma,
*PVSM, AVSM, ADC**

We are a growing Navy, of a nation with a growing economy, growing hope, growing confidence and a growing sense of the increasing role for India in world affairs. As the Navy grows, we also need to consolidate, to look at ourselves carefully, to critically examine how best to use our current resources, how to make our personnel even better tuned to the tasks for today and the missions for tomorrow.

Navy's acquisition programmes: It is a matter of immense satisfaction and pride for all of us in the Navy, and I am sure for every Indian, that our indigenous warship construction programmes are gradually maturing. We have many ships in different stages of construction and I expect the first of the

*The writer is Chief of the Naval Staff, Indian Navy.

Project 17 ships, the Shivalik, to be commissioned in the not-too-distant future. I mentioned consolidation. Let me illustrate how we are trying to consolidate on designs and incorporating incremental efficiencies into them. The Delhi class, called P-15 by us is being built in an upgraded form as Project Fifteen Alpha or P-15 Alpha. On the anvil is Project–15 Bravo version as well. Likewise, we will have the P-17A ships in due course. This consolidation enables us to have savings in cost as well as time, while still enabling improvements to be put in place. I am glad that, despite initial delays, the Scorpene submarine building line is being brought back on track. This capability will be very important for the country. We also have other classes of vessels on order. These include Naval Offshore Patrol Vessels (4+5), Anti-submarine corvettes (04), Mine Counter Measure Vessels (2+6), Fast Interceptor Craft (15+80), Water Jet FACs (10-04 delivered, 06 under construction) and Shallow Water ASW crafts (16) (DAC approval accorded). We also hope to build two Landing Platform (Dock)s indigenously, perhaps in a collaborative effort.

While the course for indigenous construction is well-charted, we also need to revisit the build strategies of our shipyards. Delays and cost-overruns in our naval shipbuilding projects with our Defence PSUs have been a better matter of great concern. A serious re-look at addressing deficiencies in warship-building methodology is considered essential at this juncture. The need for the participation of both public and private shipyards to meet the growing requirements is more than ever felt. The Navy is poised for growth, and I see it as a win-win situation for all stakeholders. We are closely following worldwide trends in warship construction technology, and our own shipyards need to infuse themselves to benchmark against world standards. The increase in fleet size and capabilities needs to match the changing warfare paradigms. We have greater national and international responsibilities commensurate with the growing stature of our country. Therefore, much as we would like to avoid resorting to imports, factors like difficulties in adhering to shipbuilding schedules have, in some cases, compelled us to place some orders overseas. You will agree that capability gaps are not acceptable. Hence, we have three follow-on Talwar class ships being built in Russia and two tankers in another yard abroad.

Vikramaditya: It is true that the project is behind the original schedule and the final cost needs to be resolved. We are working to a plan which sees delivery in 2012. The fourth round of talks by the Contract Negotiating Committee is in progress. The issue continues to be addressed at every level of bilateral contacts between Russia and India, and every effort is on to minimise the delay. As regards the carrier we are building in Kochi, work is going on satisfactorily well and over 10000 tons of steel have already gone into the hull. The carrier is expected to be commissioned in 2014. Some developmental work continues on the naval version of the Light Combat Aircraft and we are fully involved in this effort. We hope to obtain carrier compatibility for Tejas that is the Light Combat Aircraft (Navy), by 2013 or thereabouts.

Maritime surveillance: We would be inducting eight of the P-81 Poseidon Maritime Patrol Aircraft for which a contract was signed earlier this year. We have upgraded the IL-38 aircraft with the Sea Dragon combat suite. In addition, we have acquired 11 of the indigenous Dorniers and are working on a RFP for six Medium Range Maritime Reconnaissance aircraft. To enhance surveillance and attack capabilities of ships at sea, we are engaged in processing the acquisition of helicopters. We expect that pending issues with respect to the flight control systems of the ALH would be resolved to enable it to hover for Anti-submarine and Search and Rescue roles at sea. The induction process for 16 Multi-role helicopters of 12.5 ton class under a replacement programme is in the final days.

Coastal Security

It has been a year since 26/11 – the events were a stark reminder of the urgent need to focus on coastal security. As a consequence, the Government has initiated several measures, and the Navy's role of ensuring the maritime security of the country now specifically includes coastal security. It has been assigned the lead role in this endeavour, and the Coast Guard, Marine Police, intelligence, ports, immigration and offshore operators along with concerned departments of the Central and state governments, who are all stakeholders in coastal security, have been tasked to assist the Navy.

You will appreciate that the closer one gets to the shore, the larger the number of agencies involved. These include ports, fisheries, offshore operators, shipping agencies, Customs, Immigration, intelligence agencies, lighthouses and industries located along the coast. Each of these agencies has its own size of responsibility, and the major task has been to address issues of coordination. Given that the sea cannot be fenced or occupied, the management and surveillance of sea areas is a difficult and capital intensive task at best. The situation is further compounded by the density of fishing along our coasts. On any given day, we have thousands of fishing craft operating off either coast. In the past few weeks, the media has been addressing many angles of this complex issue. We are stepping up acquisition processes for hardware that is on track, and will put into place the training required to optimally use that hardware. Further, enhancing the effectiveness of multi-agency coordination has been the endeavour of all stakeholders in improving coastal security. We have carried out a series of tactical exercises on both coasts and these were particularly useful in enhancing inter-agency coordination. While they were convened by the respective naval Commanders-in-Chief, they involved state governments, Coast Guard, fisheries, port authorities, marine police many constituted recently, customs and other stakeholders. Most importantly, local coastal communities were also sensitized and energized since they play a key role as "eyes and ears" in the matrix for coastal security. The CISF and State Marine Police have important roles along the shore line, in ports and in waters very close to the shore, what could be termed as the sea-land interface. They have begun inducting some hardware and the Navy has taken on some specific training in watermanship for them. At INS Chilka, in Orissa, we have just finished training 263 CISF personnel and we will continue the programme. Hardware inductions include AIS or the Automated Identification System equipment, coastal radars to more aircraft and fast interceptor craft; measures for more effective port control; and the start of satellite-based tracking of vessels. The number and range of hardware is very large and will take a while for induction and operationalisation. We are also setting up the "Sagar Prahari Bal" which is a core group of 1000 officers and men of the Navy trained for force protection, Visit and Search duties onboard ships and ashore.

Maritime Domain Awareness: It is the term that navies now use to describe what patrolling and surveillance enable us to have: awareness of who is where; what is he doing; where is he headed. Maritime Domain Awareness (MDA) is, therefore, an all-encompassing term that involves being cognizant of the position and intentions of all actors, whether friendly, hostile or neutral, in the constantly evolving maritime environment, and in a defined area of interest. The gaps in the knowledge or awareness available at various levels is sought to be filled by surveillance, intelligence and sharing of information. MDA is a vital ingredient to a nation's, region's or indeed, the world's maritime security and is a core requirement for their economic well-being. This is achieved by networking diverse sources of information to obtain a common operational picture. High situational awareness is the prime enabler of security task across the entire range of eventualities.

The world that we know today is very different from the one that it was just a decade back. In many ways it has become a lot more unpredictable and uncertain. Amidst this twin paradigm of unpredictability and uncertainty, fundamental shifts are taking place not just in the Indian Ocean Region but globally. This is true not only of present financial condition but equally of the complex security situation. As is the case of the financial situation which necessitated a global response, the security situation is no different. Our growing maritime interests place upon the Indian Navy certain responsibilities in securing those interests.

Indian Ocean Naval Symposium

The Indian Navy has always remained at the forefront of military diplomacy and has worked towards building bridges of friendship across the oceans. Our initiatives have included MILANs at Port Blair which is attended not only by the South and SE Asian navies, but from even farther afield; International Fleet Reviews and bilateral interactions at sea with several navies. In fact, all the navies of the Indian Ocean have come together, and have formed the Indian Ocean Naval Symposium (IONS) with an aim of fostering regional cooperation in the maritime domain.

Trade-interdependence undoubtedly is our first driver that catalyses regional maritime cooperation. The Asia-Pacific region is home to some of the fastest growing economies in the world and consequently economic factors are central to this region's security concerns. The second is the Need for Energy. The continuous and assured supply of energy resources such as oil, natural gas, coal or other minerals for both the developed and developing nations in this region needs no emphasis. Any challenge to the free flow of energy resources can lead to serious consequences. Thirdly, many of the sources of terrorism with ramifications to the Indian Ocean Region and beyond, lie within the IOR. Zones of instability and violence do exist in the region and we are aware of the need to control these, not just by exercising hard power but through concurrent exercise of soft power. Fourthly, Low Intensity Maritime Conflict waged by non-state actors, cuts across state boundaries and requires cooperative, multi-national responses. With the thinning of the line between terrorism and other illegal activities, the scenario at sea has become even more complex. Other than proliferation, this has led to other unlawful activities like piracy, armed robbery or gun and drug running, all of which are or likely to be intertwined with terrorism. In the coming years, to counter the challenges posed by such threats, cooperative use of maritime forces would be required. Lastly, we must also uphold our responsibility to assist in United Nations sanctioned operations as and when they are sanctioned, whenever and wherever we can.

As I said, the IONS movement is gathering momentum. Some of you may be aware that the Chairmanship of this grouping will be passed on to the Commander of the UAE Navy for the period from 2010 to 2012. The fundamentally collective nature of this Symposium is self-evident in the theme he has chosen for the next two years, which is: "Together, for the Reinforcement of Maritime Security in the Indian Ocean." The IONS has almost three dozen member navies that bring to the table diverse capabilities and experience of operating in differing environments. Yet, issues like piracy, armed robbery, drug trafficking, terrorism to name some at one end of the violence scale or indeed, humanitarian relief consequent to natural disasters or search and rescue at other end, are ones that many navies are engaged in. In the years ahead, I am sure IONS will continue to look at collective and cooperative solutions for some of these.

Meanwhile, we continue to have a ship on patrol in the Gulf of Aden escorting merchant ships in direct coordination with the Director General Shipping. To date, over 600 ships have been escorted by us with not a single incident of hijacking in the process. We are also assisting Seychelles with periodic patrols in their Exclusive Economic Zone. Pirates have hijacked ships as far as 600 miles from the Horn of Africa and governments are rightly concerned about this. We will continue to make our contributions towards the maintenance of good order at sea that will benefit the global shipping community and oceanic commerce.

Modernisation

Our growing interests require a growing Navy. To cater for such growth plans, we also have had to put new infrastructure in place. The naval base at Karwar will undergo a second phase of expansion to augment berthing, maintenance and waterfront facilities. Our Dockyards are constantly being upgraded to keep pace with new inductions and infusion of newer technologies. To make surveillance more effective, we have commissioned some air stations and upgraded facilities at existing stations. The process continues.

Training: Let me emphasise that the greatest investment we make is in our people. They are our mainstay and their contributions are at the core of our effectiveness as an instrument of our nation. We are looking closely at further improving training and enhancing skills. We are inducting very motivated and well qualified sailors and their further training is being reshaped to cater for their increased qualifications. Officer training is undergoing a major shift with the commissioning of the new Naval Academy at Ezhimala. All cadets at the Indian Naval Academy would undergo a B Tech course for four years. We are also upgrading opportunities for SSC officers. The media have noticed that two women officers have recently earned their wings as "Observers". This means that they would be engaged in operational flying over the sea from bases ashore. As you know, the Navy has a large component of civilians who do sterling work in our shore facilities. We continue to look at building their skills and enhancing professional opportunities.

These men and women are our most vital asset. Their well-being is therefore, an important concern for the Government as well as the Navy. The Government's initiative of providing housing to the maximum number of service personnel through the Married Accommodation Project is resulting in higher satisfaction levels amongst the rank and file. Within naval stations, we are committed to providing better conditions and facilities, not only for serving personnel, but for dependents as well. These also include opportunities for spouses and widows of naval personnel to learn new skills and take up vocations.

Let me conclude by stating that the evolving maritime environment holds out many challenges and opportunities for our nation and our Navy. My focus would be to consolidate, and improve on all aspects of internal growth that shape the future Navy and contribute in every measure possible towards strengthening maritime security.

(Excerpts of Remarks of the CNS at the Navy Day Press Conference – 02 December 2009)

PENNANT NUMBERS AND NAMES OF INDIAN NAVAL SHIPS

AIRCRAFT CARRIERS

R 22	Viraat

SUBMARINES

S 73	Arihant
S 40	Vela
S 42	Vagli
S 44	Shishumar
S 45	Shankush
S 46	Shalki
S 47	Shankul
S 55	Sindhughosh
S 56	Sindhudhvaj
S 57	Sindhuraj
S 58	Sindhuvir
S 59	Sindhuratna
S 60	Sindhukesari
S 61	Sindhukirti
S 62	Sindhuvijay

S 63	Sindhurakshak
S 65	Sindhushastra

DESTROYERS

D 51	Rajput
D 52	Rana
D 53	Ranjit
D 54	Ranvir
D 55	Ranvijay
D 60	Mysore
D 61	Delhi
D 62	Mumbai

FRIGATES

F 20	Godavari
F 21	Gomati
F 22	Ganga
F 31	Brahmaputra
F 35	Udaygiri
F 36	Dunagiri
F 37	Beas
F 39	Betwa
F 40	Talwar
F 41	Taragiri
F 42	Vindhyagiri
F 43	Trishul
F 44	Tabar
F 46	Krishna (training)

CORVETTES

P 33	Abhay
P 34	Ajay
P 35	Akshay
P 36	Agray
P 44	Kirpan
P 46	Kuthar
P 47	Khanjar

P 49	Khukri
P 61	Kora
P 62	Kirch
P 63	Kulish
P 64	Karmukh
K 40	Veer
K 41	Nirbhik
K 42	Nipat
K 43	Nishank
K 44	Nirghat
K 45	Vibhuti
K 46	Vipul
K 47	Vinash
K 48	Vidyut
K 83	Nashak
K 91	Pralaya
K 92	Prabal

PATROL FORCES

P 50	Sukanya
P 51	Subhadra
P 52	Suvarna
P 53	Savitri
P 55	Sharada
P 56	Sujata

Super Dvora Mk.II ClassFAC T-80 -

FAC T-81 -
FAC T-82 -
FAC T-83 -
FAC T-84 -
FAC T-85 -
FAC T-86 -

MINE WARFARE FORCES

M 61	Pondicherry
M 62	Porbandar

M 63	Bedi
M 64	Bhavnagar
M 65	Alleppey
M 66	Ratnagiri
M 67	Karwar
M 68	Cannanore
M 69	Cuddalore
M 70	Kakinada
M 71	Kozhikode
M 72	Konkan
M 83	Mahe
M 86	Malpe

AMPHIBIOUS FORCES

L 17	Sharabh
L 18	Cheetah
L 19	Mahish
L 20	Magar
L 21	Guldar
L 22	Kumbhir
L 23	Gharial
L 34	Vasco da Gama
L 35	MK.8/MK.3 Landing craft
L 36	MK.8/MK.3 Landing craft
L 37	MK.8/MK.3 Landing craft
L 38	Midhur
L 39	Mangala
L 41	Jalashwa

AUXILIARIES AND SURVEY SHIPS

(B-561 Class)	Nicobar
(B-561 Class)	Andamans
A 15	Nireekshak
A 53	Matanga
A 57	Shakti
A 58	Jyoti
A 59	Aditya
A 72	Torpedo Recovery Vessel

A 74	Sagardhwani
A 75	Tarangini
A 86	Tir
J 14	Nirupak
J 15	Investigator
J 16	Jamuna
J 17	Sutlej
J 18	Sandhayak
J 19	Nirdeshak
J 21	Darshak
J 22	Sarvekshak
J 33	Meen
J 34	Mithun

SEAWARD DEFENCE FORCES

T 58	-
T 59	-
T 61	Trinkat
T 63	Tarasa
T 65	Bangaram
T 66	Bitra
T 67	Batti Malv
T 68	Baratang
T-69	Car Nicobar
T-70	Chetlat
T-71	Kora Divh
T-72	Cheriyam
J 33	Meen
J 34	Mithun

Chapter 10

Indian Navy by 2022

*Cmde Ranjit B Rai**

"India's growing international stature gives it strategic relevance in the area ranging from the Persian Gulf to the Straits of Malacca...India has exploited the fluidities of the emerging world order to forge new links through a combination of diplomatic repositioning, economic resurgence and military firmness".

—India's Prime Minister Dr Manmohan Singh

In support of the nation's growing strengths and responsibilities, the Indian Navy is determined to create and sustain a three dimensional, technology enabled and networked force, capable of safeguarding India's maritime interests on the high seas and projecting combat power across the littoral.

[From the Vision Statement of the Indian Navy – 2007]

---

*The writer served as Director Naval Operations and Intelligence and Commander of the Naval Academy. Presently he is a Broadcast Journalist and author of four books.

A Preamble to the Indian Navy

The Indian Navy is the fastest growing navy in the Indian Ocean and the task is cut out to ensure stability in the Indian Ocean and to provide India's nuclear deterrent from the seas, its role has been spelt out by the government. The Indian Navy is a very professional and modern force. When India attained Independence, the ethos of the Indian officers of the then Royal Indian Navy (RIN) was shaped by the traditions and professionalism of the Royal Navy which had sired and nurtured them. The Royal Navy was the pre-eminent navy of the world. The young Indian officers and men of the RIN took part in the Second World War under the Royal Ensign of Britain and became battle hardened, with many earning awards of the British Empire (MBE and OBE). The thinking of then Royal Indian Navy was succinctly brought out in the statement made by Sir Winston Churchill in the British Parliament when he was the First Lord of the Admiralty; he said "The Navy is nothing if it has no strategy", and a navy is essential for a nation to be powerful. These words were etched in the minds of officers who later went on to reach the highest ranks in the Indian Navy (IN) and included Admirals Kataria, Karmarkar (the first Indian to command British officers as a Commanding Officer), Soman Chakraverti, Chatterji, Krishnan and SM Nanda, the Chief of the Naval Staff who planned the bombing of ships at the Pakistani port of Karachi in 1971.

Lord Mountbatten, India's first Viceroy shaped the IN's expansion by an ambitious induction of ships from the UK including the aircraft carrier INS Vikrant (ex Hercules), and large cruisers like INS Delhi (HMS Achilles), famous for the Battle of the River Plate, and INS Mysore (HMS Nigeria). Therefore, the IN has always known how to handle large ships and started looking over the horizon with its burgeoning aviation arm. The IN is no stranger to strategic planning with capital ships and large fleets. Presently, Indian Navy's plans and strategy, graded from peace to war and based on providing diplomacy, humanitarian aid, constabulary and victory in war, find a prominent place in its vision statement with the Indian Ocean as its main theatre of operations. It was Alfred Thayer Mahan who prophetically predicted that the future of the 21st century lies in the waters of the Indian Ocean. No wonder the Chinese Navy has shown interest in the Indian Ocean by an expeditionary deployment of ships off Somalia to combat piracy and has crafted a 'string of pearls' strategy to build bases in the Indian Ocean Region at Gwadar in Pakistan, Humbantota in Sri Lanka and Sittwe in Myanmar.

Indian Navy's Post-Independence Record

In the 1965 India-Pakistan war, the navy was ordered not to cross the latitude of Porbandar on the Gujarat coast by a government edict but, as a fighting force in the post-Independence era, the IN had fought gallantly in the Goa Operation 'Vijay' and INS Betwa had sunk the Portuguese naval ship Afonso de Albuquerque off Goa.

In the 1971 war against Pakistan, the IN heralded missile warfare when its ships audaciously struck Karachi Port and sank three ships in the opening hours of the war and successfully blockaded East Pakistan. This led ultimately to the capitulation by Pakistan and consequently to the birth of Bangladesh. For this the credit must go to the IN planners who had turned to the then Soviet Union in the 1960s when the West shunned and enforced sanctions against India for its foreign policy of neutrality during the Cold War. On the other hand, the USA was arming Pakistan. The legendary Admiral of the Fleet Sergie Gorshkov personally ensured the supply of over 75 warships, submarines and MR aircraft including the lease of the Charlie class nuclear submarine INS Chakra (K-43) in 1987. The latter was a strategic asset and this was a precursor to India joining the nuclear club.

In the 1999 Kargil war, the combined fleets of the navy were poised to strike should there be a need, in what is known as the classical naval manoeuvre. The rescue work by the navy in December 2004 in the tsunami hit areas of South Asia was lauded the world over and the government and the nation appreciated the navy's capabilities.

The Indian Navy Today and Foreign Acquisitions

The fact that the IN has only been able to achieve the force level of only 118 ships, 16 aging submarines and 150 aging aircrafts and helicopters with a personnel strength of 52,000; this is because of the budget constraints. The security of India's land borders has always been the focus of the government's defence policy. Post Independence, India's defence strategy was shaped by a continental outlook and remained Pakistan-centric for far too long and many call this lack of maritime support as 'sea blindness' but now this is changing.

The IN now has 40 ships on order including two aircraft carriers, six modern conventional submarines and a long line of combatant platforms, MR aircraft, helicopters and two nuclear submarines— one indigenous and one Akula class from Russia. The navy—mandated to provide India's nuclear deterrent from the seas— has converted two OPVs (INS Subhadra and Sukanya) to fire the 350 km nuclear-capable Dhanush missile made by the DRDO and each OPV can carry two missiles for vertical launch. India's engineering company Larsen and Toubro has contributed to this launching system and is now standard for all future missile launchers. These OPV platforms will be augmented with India's home-built Advanced Technology Vessels (ATVs), a pseudonym for India's home-built nuclear submarines, the first of which the 6000 ton INS Arihant was launched by Mrs Gursharan Kaur—wife of the prime minister—on 26 July 2009 at the Ship Building Centre (SBC) at Vishakhapatnam. The prime minister was present on this occasion besides the Russian Ambassador in India who was present with a large contingent of Russian technicians. After a year's harbour trials the boat will join the fleet in 2011 with eight DRDO designed Sagarika, under-water vertical launcher for 700 km nuclear-tipped missile. When that is accomplished, the Indian Navy can be proud of the technological achievement.

The Navy is on track to commission the 44,000 ton aircraft carrier INS Vikramaditya (Admiral Gorshkov) with 16 MiG-29Ks by 2013, and three Yantar built Krivak frigates from 2011 with pre-installed supersonic BrahMos cruise missiles, all from Russia. All IN front-line ships and future conventional submarines will have the supersonic 300 km range BrahMos missiles. A modern multi-purpose tanker-cum-logistics supply vessel will also join the fleet by 2011 from Fincantieri in Italy and a repeat order for another has been placed. The navy has ordered 8 P8i Boeing MR aircraft and is on track to order six MRMR aircrafts and 12 ASW helicopters from abroad to boost its maritime surveillance at sea.

The Navy Exercises and Innovations

Lately, the US Navy and other navies have opened their portholes to the Indian Navy. The officers and men of the navy have gained immensely by the exposure to the USN and NATO hardware and tactical procedures by stints at the Norfolk US base and in the exercises at Malabar (with the USN), Varuna (with France) and Konkan (with the Royal Navy) involving advanced manoeuvres. IN ships have operated in net-centric interoperable conditions with large US aircraft carriers, nuclear submarines and advanced MR aircraft like the P 3-C Orions in 13 Malabar exercises in waters as far as Okinawa in Japan, the South China seas and with Japanese MSDF, along with the Australian and Singapore Navy ships in what was called the QUAD. The operational and technological exposure for the next generation personnel of the navy has been truly rewarding and the young officers of the Weapons Engineering and Electronics Systems Establishment (WEESE) have enabled the Indian Navy to become net-enabled with internet protocols at sea with digital modems based on ARINC 249. The digital data can be transmitted by INMARSAT, HF and VHF with Link II equipment, based on USN's CENTRIX, indigenously manufactured by Bharat Electronics Ltd (BEL) with software from Tata Consultancy Ltd. Over 148 sets have been supplied to ships, helicopters, naval headquarters, commands and the Flag Officer Defence Advisory Group at Mumbai. In the near future ISRO will provide the navy with a dedicated satellite with ship-based Ku/Ka terminals to be even more net-enabled and connected 24×7. The Indian Navy is one of the first to take control of shore launched Heron and Searcher UAVs from ships at sea by providing two Leander platforms INS Taragiri and Vindhyagiri control containers on board, and is in the hunt for a ship based UAV like the Firescout.

The Futuristic Indian Navy and Coast Guard

It is no surprise therefore the spotlight has been on the Indian Navy as one of the fastest growing navies in the region. According to the former Chief of Naval Staff Admiral Sureesh Mehta, the IN's front line fleet by 2022 will include three aircraft carrier groups, over forty large combatant platforms and submarines, with a capability for ocean-wide surveillance, sea control and be a fully net-centric force, for which the templates have been cut. This includes three Shivalik class with INS Shivalik the first in November 2000, and there is a follow-up plan for seven stealth frigates to be built (four at MDL and three at GRSE) for Rs 45,000 crores ($ 11 billion) as approved by the Defence Acquisition Council. The platforms now building in India besides Shivalik class three Klub missiles-fitted frigates, three BrahMos missile-fitted destroyers (Type 15A), six Scorpene submarines (at MDL) and four 3000 ton Naval OPVs at Goa Shipyard Ltd. In a unique experiment, Alcock Ashdown at Bhavnagar is constructing six 600 ton Catamaran survey ships of the Austal design with organic helicopters and the first will be commissioned in 2010. Cochin Shipyard Ltd is building the 37,500 ton STOBAR indigenous aircraft carrier and GRSE at Kolkata is building fast attack craft and four Project 28 ASW Corvettes. The navy is to build six OPVs in India with foreign collaboration.

The navy has also made plans to induct large platforms which will double the landing operations, flag showing and for benign and humanitarian missions in the region. Based on the

2004 tsunami experience when the Indian Navy came to the rescue of its neighbours with alacrity, the Indian Navy acquired the 17,500 ton second-hand LPD INS Jalashwa (Trenton) with 6 Sikorsky second-hand Seaking helicopters under the US FMS maintenance scheme which provides the operational availability.

Post 26/11, the attack in Mumbai by sea-borne Pak-based terrorists the Indian Navy has now been charged to oversee the coastal security and the Indian Coast Guard is also gearing up for expansion as the nation's guardian of the shores and its littoral, to maintain order in our EEZ which promises to be the supplier of food and mineral resources in the 21st century. The Coast Guard has three OPVs under construction at Goa Shipyard Ltd and has approval for seven more in India under a global tender. A large number of small fast crafts are under construction also for inshore coastal patrol.

Today, drilling and excavation at ultradeep depths is a technological reality and India has been allotted 150,000 sq miles of space in the Indian Ocean to exploit the sea bed under the Laws of the Seas (UNCLOS) enterprise and the ministry of science and technology has laid the foundation for this. In war, the coast guard with 75 ships and 45 aircrafts and helicopters comes under the navy, thus augmenting its capabilities. The Prime Minister Dr Manmohan Singh speaking at the annual commanders conference in 2006 appreciated the role of the navy and coast guard in the 21st Century, and assured the navy that funds would not be a constraint for its expansion. The realization has dawned that only the nations with adequate maritime capabilities can meet the threats to the nation.

The maritime template of India has articulated the Indian Navy's strategy document, and the navy's top brass have categorically expressed for a mission denominated capability based approach to force planning in a classified document 'Maritime Capability Perspective Plan-2022'. In unclassified terms the navy has also issued a Maritime Doctrine so essential for any force to operate. Earlier the government had approved the 15-year shipbuilding plan and to set up a two line 30-year submarine building programme. As Lord Admiral Cunningham said in the 1940s, it takes 10 years to build ships and 100 to build a navy. It is now possible to compress time for building warships with modular construction, and fortunately the Indian Navy has many years of sea going and modest war fighting experience in their blood to operate warships.

The Indian Navy has a unique 350 strong corps of naval constructors, a specialist arm of the engineering branch that celebrated its golden jubilee on 17 November 2006. Officers of the corps and the WESEE have contributed to ship and submarine designs, repair and maintenance, innovations in EW, radars, and designed CICs and the Link II network interface. WESEE has contributed to the missile programmes and R&D in naval research institutions. The navy outsources projects to universities for its crypto needs and technical officers are encouraged to take postgraduate degrees for their mid-career progress. Many who have left the navy hold key posts in the software and technology industries of India, which have blossomed. This has been the navy's contribution to the nation, a sequel of navy's indigenous shipbuilding plans. These achievements have not been applauded. It is akin to the world famous company Lever Brothers who train personnel not only for profits but also release talent to the nation.

Explaining the navy's vision, former CNS Admiral Mehta stated, "India aims to ensure a secure and peaceful environment in the Indian Ocean Region and to further India's political, economic, diplomatic and military objectives are the navy's responsibilities. We will deter conflict through conventional and non-conventional strength. But if this fails, we will fight to achieve decisive victory over our adversaries." In the given scenario no one can ignore terrorism, nuclear proliferation and threat of weapons of mass destruction. Mehta was clear that the navy's security concerns would span all forms of conflicts from low-end to nuclear threshold. India is cooperating with China but its military power will be competitive in the years ahead. He further stated, "The risk of conventional conflict also looms large over the subcontinent. Therefore, we expect our neighbours to operate on all spectrums of conflicts. Threats are many—transient and dynamic."

Conclusion

The Navy has been successfully operating UAVs and Dornier 228s for MDA. In future the Indian Air Force will also be a strategic force multiplier for the Navy in the IOR with its mid-air refuellers, the Phalcon AEW&C aircraft and satellite assets like the Israeli built synthetic aperture RISAT-2 radar satellite and the air launched 290 km supersonic BrahMos missile. The ex Air Chief Fali Major has often stressed the technological advancements in the Indian Air Force (IAF) that have made it a strategic force. As the fourth largest air force in the world and with the government's support in terms of acquisitions, and infrastructure build-up, the IAF has a bright future, and has taken on the responsibility to manage the assets and capabilities of the IAF in the changed security scenario in the region. The IAF plans to accomplish its primary aim to deliver aerospace power, whenever and wherever required, including in the Indian Ocean.

In the process of globalisation and integration and multi-literalism, the navy's plans are catering to the new found responsibilities thrust on it as it cooperates with China in trade, but keeps a watchful eye on China's strategic reach and intentions in the Indian Ocean. The senior echelon of the IN have imitated comprehensive actions of past maritime powers with out of the box thinking, and taken advantage of the global economy and shed non-alignment, post the cold war. This caused a shift in the balance of power giving an edge to India over Pakistan with regard to Indian Ocean. In the wake of this India's strategy is no longer Pakistan-centric or reactive. In the last ten years, despite the current downturn, the world has witnessed an unprecedented economic transformation which is bound to have long-term repercussions on India's future and in that India's maritime aspirations have been flagged in this paper. The geopolitics in the Indian Ocean hold many keys to portray how India will fare while the scenario is still unfolding. A recent quote by Admiral Sureesh Mehta at the Shangrila dialogue and list of acquisitions is as follows:

"We see the Indian Navy as a significant stabilising force in the Indian Ocean region, which safeguards traffic bound not only for our own ports, but also the flow of hydrocarbons and strategically important cargo to and from the rest of the world across the strategic waterways close to our shores. And so, the safety of SLOCS will always remain a priority for India in the foreseeable future".

List of major Combatants as in 2009 on Order and being planned for 2017 – ORBAT of the Indian Navy. 165 warships plus 400 air platforms	
Type of Platform	Ordered/ Planned
Aircraft Carrier 40-year-old INS "Viraat" with Sea Harriers till 2014. 8 MR Boeings P8i ordered. 6 MRMR Planes and 12 ASW Helicopters to be ordered.	2 Carriers Gorshkov and ADS with MiG-29Ks by 2013–14
Landing Pontoon Dock (LPD) INS "Jalshawa" acquired FMS Route from USA	1/New Design Under selection
Destroyers 3 "Type 15A" plus 3 "Kashin" BrahMos Upgrades. INS Rajput and INS Ranvir Upgraded with VLS BrahMos and Barak AA system	3-15A+ 3 Destroyers
Frigates 3 "Krivack" in Russia. 3 "Type 17" at MDL India. Plus new design sought for six Frigates. One to be built abroad rest in India. MCM and DSRVs	6/6 being examined and MCM also in final selection
4 ASW Corvettes Type 28 and 6 FACs. Six Survey Ships of Austal Catamaran design	4 Type 28+6 FACS +6 Survey Catamarans
Offshore Patrol Vessels (OPV) / New Naval Design	5/ plus 6 LOI

Chapter 11

IAF— Future Aerospace Power

Air Chief Marshal PV Naik,
*PVSM, AVSM, ADC**

"I see a future, where the Indian Air Force will project aerospace power credibly, within its zone of influence with precision, speed and high intensity, against a variety of objectives."

Over the last year, our operational preparedness has remained at an all time high. Numerous operational tasks that stretched our resources were successfully completed. Today the prevailing situation is such that we have to maintain a certain level of constant readiness.

A large number of acquisitions like the MMRCA, helicopters, FRAs, AWACS and transport aircraft will be in place in the next few years. They will provide a quantum leap to the IAF's

*The writer is Chief of the Air Staff, Indian Air Force.

operational capability. While new inductions are following one after another, present systems have got to carry on. A great responsibility lies on all of us, to ensure that while we absorb new technology, we continue operating all current systems, effectively and efficiently.

The first AWACS aircraft is with the Indian Air Force and is in the process of operational induction. This induction is going to change the very manner that we operate, both in terms of offensive as well as defensive operations.

Air Maintenance of Army and other paramilitary personnel is continuing, especially in the Northern and Eastern sectors. The AF airlifts more than 37,000 tonnes annually towards Air Maintenance. Aid to civil power by the IAF transport and helicopter fleets has progressively increased over the years. This year, the IAF has flown more than 600 sorties and airlifted more than 400 tonnes of material towards relief operations.

To further military diplomacy and for addressing issues of inter-operability, IAF continues with a series of international exercises. This month itself, we are involved in two international exercises. Our fighters are going to Oman for a bilateral air exercise, while a component of the US transport fleet is coming for Ex-Cope India – 09. There has been a substantial growth in Defence Cooperation activities with a host of countries.

We are maintaining our three aviation contingents, two in Congo and one in Sudan. The professional competence of air warriors in these peace-keeping missions has been acknowledged at the highest levels by various Force Commanders and the highest offices of the UN.

During the past few years, the IAF has made rapid strides towards attaining net centricity. Security of our cyber assets, therefore, will be of paramount importance. We have to take all possible steps to preserve the integrity of our systems.

I see a future, where the Indian Air Force will project aerospace power credibly, within its zone of influence with precision, speed and high intensity, against a variety of objectives. The IAF has to be capable of dominating the entire spectrum of information, cyberspace and airspace so that we can conduct operations, efficiently, and on our terms.

The professionalism and competence of the Indian Air Force is acknowledged world wide, and the Nation can be justifiably proud of it. I assure all Indians of the IAF's capability and its commitment. As Air Warriors, we re-dedicate ourselves to the service of the Nation and renew our pledge to do our sovereign duty – "with honour and pride" and indeed "Touch the Sky with Glory."

(Excerpts of the Address by the Chief of Air Staff on Air Force Day 2009 on 08 October 2009)

Chapter 12

The Indian Air Force in Transition

*Air Chief Marshal Fali Homi Major, PVSM, AVSM, SC, VM**

Countries need the sum of their National power to progress. Military power is a very critical component of this National power, without which, progress is possible only up to the point where it clashes with the interests of another stronger Nation. Events of the past two decades and recent research suggest that aerospace power has increasingly become a very crucial part of this military power and the preferred instrument of choice to address conventional and sub-conventional crises situations. It alone possesses the ability to reach from above and outside, with control over the process of escalation as well as disengagement. The seemingly isolated actions of an aviator have far-reaching strategic implications. Every action or inaction, of an element of airpower highlights a country's will and intent.

*The writer retired as Chief of the Air Staff, Indian Air Force.

The decision to use airpower in a conflict situation makes a very powerful statement. In our own context, whilst the Kargil incursions by Pakistan were definitely news, they grabbed world attention only after the use of airpower. Such an act invariably demonstrates the resolve of the political leadership. Interestingly, a very different effect was illustrated with the Indian Air Force action, of not crossing the LC. Arguably, that such an act, one that demonstrated restraint, in contradiction to tactical propriety, actually paid greater dividends in the form of gaining favour in the world opinion and ultimate achievement of our national objective; that of evicting the intruders.

Employment of airpower usually has an effect, far in excess of its application. Knowingly or unknowingly, airpower has also been a tool of foreign policy. The response of the British to the appearance of the Gotha bombers over London in 1919 was far in excess of the actual threat. The deployment of these aircrafts was a statement by the German High Command and went on to create a fear psychosis and uproar among the British. Suggestively, it shaped and affected foreign policy decisions and influenced thinking, even until the end of the Second World War. At its core, airpower involves access to a realm of nature to the long exclusion of human beings. Control and superiority in this sphere, not necessarily in conflict alone, automatically places a nation in a position of pre-eminence, giving it power. It seems to hint at an underlying force and competence, which sometimes makes the difference in a bargaining situation.

In the light of an expanding strategic footprint of a resurgent India and the need therefore, to safeguard its National interests, the IAF must have a credible and demonstrable capability to operate effectively and decisively, right up to its extremities. The profound influence that aerospace power has, given its inherent speed, flexibility, reach, stealth, precision and ubiquity make it the natural instrument of choice to address conventional and sub-conventional conflict situations, as well as force projection. The IAF therefore, need to be structured, equipped and trained to do this and more.

Modernization

It is axiomatic that armed forces must prepare only for capabilities and not intentions. Given India's concerns and aspirations, a strong and comprehensive aerospace capability is inescapable. IAF's modernization plan must therefore, aim to sustain and enhance its operational potential and consolidate the specified force levels through judicious and cost-effective replacements and up gradation of existing resources. It must be a gradual, but transformational modernization.

How the IAF must evolve, compare it with any other evolving air force and the path charted by the advanced air forces, there are essential similarities. Since aerospace power, its capabilities, effectiveness, and indeed its utility depend on technology, which in turn is a dependant operational need, all air forces would envision evolving on similar lines. In fact, but for minor variations, the IAF is on a globally recognized growth path. Therefore, depending upon the circumstances, threat perceptions and resources, it is the scope and pace of growth of the IAF that essentially remains to be determined.

Clearly, the IAF must be equipped for long-reach, persistence, precision targeting, and air dominance, networked and space-enabled capabilities. This requires hardware, organization and people. The hardware must be well chosen and procured in time; the organization must be adaptive; and the people must be competent, motivated and well trained. What flows from this must be an action plan, but what is most important is actualizing this plan. The acquisition, upgrade and infrastructure build-up plans of the IAF are in public domain. The IAF has to achieve these plans in the three-plan period up to 2020.

Much will also depend upon the way aerospace power develops in the future. Beyond the MMRCA and FGFA, with their 40-year life, we need to think beyond 2060. It is not easy to guess the shape and complexity of aerospace power so far ahead: would the accent shift to unmanned flight, to missiles or would 'air' be more of 'space'? Despite the unpredictability, it is certain that the need for application and transportability of National power through aerospace power would continue. Nations that lack it will seek it. Aerospace power is bound to proliferate and permeate the National security apparatus more completely, including for homeland security. The IAF will seek greater specialization; tailored capabilities, an increased dependence on unmanned vehicles and greater accent on force enhancers.

Space-based assets and defensive counter-space measures will be the way forward, since a quiet space race is already a global reality, with a distinct possibility of weaponisation. Perhaps more than any other, it is aerospace power, which is the most significant. In addition, the integration of space-enabled capabilities will enhance the aerospace power. Evolving into an aerospace force is thus a logical progression. However, it is getting crowded up there and we need to act fast. Although space empowers all Services, the IAF must be the leader. Any fledgling capability requires residing in an appropriate parent capability. Air power, or the IAF, is the closest such capability or organization, suitable to host and nurture military space. India's rising status and acceptability are an opportunity for us to push for creating an adequate military space capability.

Since IAF requires a comprehensive capability, its future in the long-term, will largely mirror the future of aerospace power itself. However, the interests of the leading nations have profound influence over this path; India must be selective and seek creative variations, both in terms of hardware and doctrine.

Technological Challenges

There is no doubt that aerospace power will be the primary option and instrument of choice in any future conflict. Technology is the premise of the projection and application of the aerospace power. Acquiring and assimilating this technology are going to be the two biggest challenges for the Indian Air Force.

The lack of it will curtail National options, affecting postures and doctrines. Denial and selective availability from other countries will always create complications in international relations. Therefore, indigenization of core aerospace technologies must become a National quest. No nation can claim to be a major power without a high level of autonomous and innovative technological capability, and a capacity to meet basic defence needs indigenously. Presently, foreign vendors are the main source of almost 70 per cent of our military hardware. As a growing economy with immense intellectual capability and industrial capacity, depending so heavily on imports in the defence sector, speaks very poorly about Defence R&D and PSUs. Given the urgent requirement to modernize our armed forces, it would make immense economic, military and social sense if the government takes immediate measures to boost indigenous capability by energizing and infusing some fresh vigour in the DRDO and PSUs.

Another characteristic that exemplifies the nature of technology today is the rate of change. Shelf lives of existing technologies are becoming shorter; hence, the newer technologies are overtaking at a breath-taking pace. This fact has a direct implication on the modernization process. The development cycle of a product from the design stage to operationalisation has to reduce; otherwise, the equipment runs the risk of becoming obsolete in its entirety. This certainly cannot happen in the IAF, given the security scenario in the neighbourhood. The question that needs answering is what should IAF do? There is a need to identify and develop core technologies for aggressive designing and manufacturing. If IAF does not carry it out in time, the country runs the risk of outside investments that will not add value to our existing state and deny us the opportunity to be self-reliant.

We need to focus into our design and development activities. The DRDO may not agree, but they cannot design, develop and manufacture all defence requirements. In the modern competitive environment, such practice is simply not cost effective, and Nations the world over are learning from the benefits of collaboration. There has to be a better and more effective way to focus research and design activities in the country. Whilst the prevalent structures and organizations have served satisfactorily over the years and brought the country to its present technological standard, it is time to evolve with changing requirements and advancing technology.

Most of the other countries undertake research and development activities in coordination with government and universities. This is not the case with us, where R&D for military equipment is mostly restricted to defence laboratories. There is need to shift defence research from the public to the private sector, and into the capable minds and hands of young scientists and entrepreneurs.

The concepts of time-bound processes, the ability to scrap a process if it does not meet the desired objective, the ability to take risks and timely decisions, are some truths, that we could do well to absorb. Another crucial area is the requirement to increase user interface in the design process. It exists to some extent, but it has to take on a more intrusive and effective role. Industry must always translate user requirements into viable technical options. The user must always remain the captain. The last two decades have resulted in a comparative surge in aerospace industry in the country. This is an encouraging sign but if unregulated, it runs the risk of wasteful expenditure and duplication of effort. There is therefore a definite need for an apex agency, to coordinate and regulate the activities of the many organs and provide a focus to develop a coherent and comprehensive National aerospace capability.

Operational and Organizational Challenges

With increasing use of technology, emerge new playgrounds of conflict. They create new vulnerabilities and new rules of engagement, requiring a different genre of war-fighting wherewithal. These constitute strange unexplored arenas, and are subject to new principles of war and yet undiscovered tactics. Worms, Trojans and Masquerades are replacing the smart weapons; seeking new targets in communications and network systems, the denial of which can be equally devastating to the overall campaign. These new battlefields form uncharted territory, add to the conventional ones already existing, and demand an entirely new set of skills and equipment. Technology in an air force largely dictates capability. Indeed, one could go so far as to say that technology is the core driver of an aerospace power. Along with the abilities and capabilities that advancements in technology provide, are also the vulnerabilities generated alongside. The very factor responsible for increasing one's capability naturally becomes a target for the adversary. Implicit in attaining a capability is an understanding that its denial is also a consequence and hence sets in motion yet another chain of never-ending, cause and effect. Space, cyberspace, urban warfare and the information domain have emerged as new battle-spaces. These demand serious attention. There are probably many others, yet unknown, that would emerge. They obviously need very different sets of equipment, tactics and warriors to carry forward the battle. The IAF needs to predict and define the emergence of these new arenas and develop capabilities to dominate them as well. Battle-space leaves no vacuum. Domination will remain with the agency that makes its first inroads and develops these capabilities. The IAF needs to be on constant lookout for new emerging battle-spaces and prepare for them.

Possession of assets alone, do not automatically translate them into capabilities. Making the right use of the equipment by generating suitable tactics, doctrine and training will decide the eventual outcome. This process will have its own gestation cycle. Every weapon system, once acquired, will need time to settle in, followed by trials, development and exploitation phase. The IAF cannot wish away this cycle. The methods of the adversary, in the face of these changes, will continue to be dynamic and demand rapid responses. This is an operational imperative, and is to be accepted. Maintaining and utilizing the newly acquired equipment needs training, this in turn, requires infrastructure and additional equipment, in a typical snowballing process. The organization needs to identify personnel, plan their profiles, and position them accordingly. The very pattern of fresh training itself will undergo modifications to cater to the new requirements. It is essential that this process must remain relevant and co-incident with the acquisition and modernization plan of the IAF.

The next major challenge is to manage the organization during these times of change. Even a cursory appreciation of the present state of the Indian Air Force will reveal that almost every bit of its inventory is undergoing some form of transformation or the other. IAF is inducting or upgrading, replacing or putting to use in an entirely new environment. Absorbing the new incoming technologies, whilst managing the existing inventories, in their entirety of maintenance, operations, training etc in this time of large-scale inductions, phase-outs and up gradations present a unique set of challenges. Traditional methods of employment and maintenance will have to coexist even as, inducing new forms and methods, often in vastly different environments. Processes that work at varying speeds will create mutual friction and interference, and will demand management skills of a very different kind.

Every organization, including the IAF has inertia. It tends to gravitate towards established patterns and, in fact, looks for traditional and time-honoured methods. Its leadership must address the exacting demands of technological change and balance it with present requirements. The challenge lies in setting up a responsive organization.

Conclusion

The Indian Air Force is poised at the threshold of a transformational change. It is also a moment of great opportunity.

The changes have marked the present age at a rate, which is unprecedented in human history. In the present scenario, time is a weapon. Whilst the concept is not new, domination and control over the temporal, assumes an altogether different dimension. It throws up challenges in the quest for enhanced capabilities and addressing these challenges constantly will keep the IAF leadership busy in the years to come.

The future, as always, remains uncertain and one can only make informed presumptions. The requirement to create an appropriately responsive organization, managing processes that move in different operational environments and speeds, and seamlessly integrate all these requirements of acquisition, employment and training are the major challenges facing the Indian Air Force, as it establishes itself during these years of transition. If the IAF is successful in establishing firm foundations at this moment, it will put it on a trajectory that will take it a generation ahead. This will also require a 'whole of government' approach and an extraordinary amount of integration, wisdom, a dash of patriotism and a total absence of parochialism amongst the many stakeholders of the National Security apparatus.

Chapter 13

India's Aeronautic Industry: Opportunities and Challenges

Air Marshal SR Deshpande,
*PVSM, AVSM, VM (G)**

In May 2001, the Government of India announced the first set of major policy changes to give stimulus to India's stagnating defence industry. The basic reasoning for these changes was firstly, to bring in the private sector and secondly, facilitate the entry of foreign companies to infuse state-of-the-art technology in the defence industry. Most International defence companies were not interested as the terms including the FDI limited to 26 per cent, were possibly not good enough for them. However, with the release of global tenders during the last few years the

---

*The writer is a former Air Officer Commanding-in-Chief, South Western Air Command. He is a Defence Analyst and Advisor in the Aerospace/Aeronautics Industry; Avionics and Weapons Technology and Military Leadership.

SU 30 of the IAF displaying at Aero India 2009. Photo Source: PIB

scene has completely changed for several big-ticket defence programmes with the policy changes vide DPP 2006, 2008 and 2009.

In the process, the overseas defence companies are showing keen interest in our acquisition programmes and in particular aeronautics industry. India's long term defence planning and investments in aeronautics sector are now at a critical point. For Indian defence planners and equally for the private sector it is time of great opportunity but also of formidable challenges.

In this article, we will discuss what the technological and business challenges are ahead of our Public and Private sectors. These changes seem linked with the force structure and operational preparedness of the Indian Air Force.

Unique Business Opportunity

To begin with, a close look at the global security scenario indicates that it has changed substantially over the past 15–20 years. In the face of new and complex multiple threats, the roles, structure and doctrine of the armed forces are undergoing corresponding changes.

In parallel, the global defence industry has also significantly evolved. They are developing new weapon systems to meet the changing operational requirements of the armed forces. From the business angle, defence companies are now going transnational needing to attract customers in a very competitive international market, forcing the companies to reform and restructure.

If we want to reap the benefits of our massive acquisition plans, then we need to fine-tune our industrial strategy suitably. The first challenge consists of designing right policies and executing them on a fast track to attract not only the Indian private sector but also investments and technologies from the overseas. It is a long awaited opportunity to transform our defence industrial base into one capable of state-of-the-art products, services and facilities.

Any wavering at this critical juncture will have a serious impact on the nation's aeronautics industry future and our aspirations to be a global player in the aeronautics industry. If we do not take the right steps now, India will take a backseat by merely purchasing the weapon systems produced by other nations and at best license-producing, as we have been doing for the past several decades.

In all these developments, the Indian Air Force has a very vital stake. Right now it is in the midst of substantial transformation, involving a series of major new programmes such as MMRCA-fourth generation combat aircraft, modern transport aircraft, helicopters, airborne early warning and control systems, flight refuellers, UAVs, smart standoff weapons, EW systems, simulation systems and modernization of airfields— in essence, refurbishing the entire fabric and structure of the air force. An estimated over 100 billion dollars will be spent on the procurement for the armed forces in the next ten years.

We expect these platforms and systems to have very long life cycles. This means the future business for the industry in many sectors will be mainly in sustaining and upgrading these platforms and systems. It would involve speedily integrating new technology to meet emerging threats to fulfil new operational requirements and not immediately moving to design the next generation systems.

Roles and Missions

Against this background, the air force missions are to deal with the potential threats. Until now, there has been general perception that the IAF is predominantly a tactical air force with limited strategic capability. The air force aims to build an inventory that would be truly a continental force capable of taking care of the following roles and missions:

- Air defence or control of the air
- Offensive counter air strike
- Counter surface or tactical strike
- Force multiplication through EW, AWACS and flight refuelling
- Protection of economic resources as well as our offshore island territories
- Counter terrorism tasks
- Strategic mobility and reach
- Power projection
- Relief operations during national disasters
- UN peacekeeping and enforcement operations

Force Structure Planning

To fulfil these roles the air force planners today have a wide range of options to build a balanced force structure and organize

Dhruv ALH helicopter flying during Aero India 2009. Photo Source: PIB

their force level to meet the perceived threats during peace and war. However, despite the advent of high technology, force structure planning and its updating usually become formidable challenges due to a few complex issues like:

- Budgetary constraints—air force acquisition plans being particularly capital intensive
- Differing bureaucratic and finance staff viewpoints
- Delays in approvals of programmes, and
- The pressure to support the DPSUs which are unable to deliver the products with requisite QRs

Thus, we had no option but to go to the external sources of supply whether the platforms, systems or even subsystems, to ensure induction of specified weapon systems.

We should not seek to restrict the scope for international cooperation and competition where this is appropriate. Military technical collaboration has emerged as an integral part of the global cooperation regime. From technology point of view, we are not at all ready to follow indigenously, a complete cradle-to-grave production in all areas. However, the new programmes give our industry an opportunity to absorb and master innovative technologies to take the industry expertise to a higher level.

If we want indigenous industry to grow, we also have to share with the private sector which technologies and capabilities we need for our future weapon programmes. Then, the private sector would be in a position to seek these technologies by way of either foreign collaboration or in-house R&D if they have the technology expertise and infrastructure.

Industrial Roadmap

To develop an effective and efficient industry base we urgently need to launch a well thought outroad map to guide the aeronautics programmes of the nation through the next industrial cycle of about 20–25 years. We must formulate a comprehensive national aeronautics policy with the core objective to promote speedy growth of aeronautics industry and create high level of competency in military aeronautics.

Key Parameters

Key parameters of the National Aeronautics Policy must substantially address the following important areas:

- *Leadership:* There is only one customer in defence business—that is the government. It must take forceful initiative and take lead in restructuring the aeronautics industry.

- *Vision:* Provide a clear and compelling vision that will drive decisions and priorities for the future of domestic aeronautics research and programmes—a vision that, once set, the government will adhere to for years to come and avoid fanciful reversals or changes.

HAL's Light Combat Aircraft Tejas at Aero India 2009.
Photo source: Rahuldevnath

- *Synergy:* Develop and implement a process whereby the government consults both public and private sectors on long-term defence planning and are participants in centrally funded programmes comprising weapon systems and equipment.
- *Infrastructure:* Ensure that cost-effective, state-of-the-art national test facilities are available to private sector to participate in aeronautics research programmes.
- *Programmes:* Pursue aeronautics research in selected advanced platforms and systems while ensuring a plan for timely transfer of these research results to the industry.
- *Human Resources:* Build up a workforce on education in aerospace engineering, software technology and science disciplines that are critical to the aeronautics sector.

Business Environment

We have a well-established public sector aeronautics industrial base. It has a broad range of capabilities, which deliver indigenous as well as license production aircraft and equipment to the air force. The LCA, ALH and other programmes have given good stimulus to SME base in private sector.

We have strong base in finance, business, marketing and IT services with a highly skilled and flexible work force.

MOD now welcomes overseas investment and plans to increase FDI to 49 per cent selectively. Offset business plan would facilitate technology transfer, additional employment and greater export potential.

However, there is a flip side to doing business in India. In a recent report of World Bank's International Finance Corporation, we are at 122nd position even below our neighbours—Nepal, Bangladesh and Pakistan due to:

- Inefficient enforcement of contracts
- Archaic bankruptcy laws
- Endless delays in issuing approvals and construction permits
- Lack of online remitting payment facility.

These issues are serious enough for the concerned government agencies to take urgent action. In addition, considering India's high GDP growth potential and volume of economy, India can overcome these drawbacks by making appropriate corrections in business administration.

Human Resource

Here, I would like to make a special mention of the potential role of defence services officers in propping up our defence industry. Services officers have extensive and in-depth knowledge of military tactics and strategy, modern weapons technologies, electronics, munitions and logistics systems. This domain knowledge is very essential within the industry to understand the intricacies of user requirements.

Unfortunately, the government neglects this talented group after their release or retirement from the service due to lukewarm attitude despite the resettlement institutions. Elsewhere in the world, the defence companies due to their 'hands-on' experience in operational, maintenance and logistics procedures seek after them. The government should value their talent to employ this capable, disciplined and dedicated set of work force in the defence industry.

Key Industrial Capabilities

To build a strong self-governing aeronautics industrial base, besides existing competencies, it would be essential to have the following capabilities at much advanced level. I will not go in details but briefly highlight few important ones.

Systems Engineering and Integration

Since the new platforms the government is inducting into service are getting increasingly complex and are likely to remain in our inventory for decades, advanced systems integration capability is very essential. To exploit and attain proficiency the government should introduce these into the existing system. This demands a high degree of systems engineering and integration skills at major component and sub-component levels. Since the subsystems are important enablers to deliver platforms capability, this would often be the route to upgrade capability and to sustain it through the total technical life of the equipment.

Fixed wing

We are ready to introduce two new, highly sophisticated manned combat jets; MMRCA in the near future and fifth generation fighter in the long term and we want both these to last for more than 40 years. Frankly, I do not visualize India needing to design and build a future generation of manned fast jet aircraft beyond these two types. However, since the new types we are introducing are likely to have long operational life, we need to achieve the ability to maintain and upgrade these types over an extended period.

Some of the critical mission systems for the future needs are electro-optical (EO) sensors; Hi-tech Radars—AESA and Conformal SAR; Electronic Support Measures (ESM); ECM Systems, precision weapons, secure data and communication systems. We need to develop competence in these areas, where the Indian industry may have to team up with foreign prime contractors for developing new solutions.

Helicopters

Helicopters, which are inherently flexible platforms and contribute to a variety of military tasks, will be an essential constituent of a balanced expeditionary force. Thanks to the success of ALH, even if it is moderate, we have accumulated a high degree of knowledge related to the rotary wing technology. ALH or Dhruv has great business potential but in a strong competitive international market, we will have to employ an aggressive marketing drive to achieve a reasonable target.

Our approach should be to invest in the future light-combat Helicopter currently undergoing detailed capability study to meet our attack and reconnaissance roles and sustain the necessary design authority at HAL in the short to medium-term. HAL also should delegate different levels of supply chain capability to private companies such as rotor blades, mission systems, vibration management and electronic architecture.

Precision Weapons

Smart Weapons provide Indian Air Force with battle winning precision effects. This will present a substantial challenge to the industry, as we have virtually no base for manufacturing new generation precision munitions; air-to-air short range and BVR missiles, glide bombs and rockets. We have to further exploit and apply our success in the Brahmos cruise missile in similar weapon derivatives. As a long-term goal, we must attain the ability to design, develop and upgrade these complex weapons

Kaveri engine being developed for LCA Tejas by DRDO.
Photo source: DRDO

in our laboratories. This is a challenging task requiring a number of critical and sensitive subsystems based on technologies such as EO, IR Imaging, guidance and control, material and warheads.

NCW Capability

The net-centric capability has today become a buzzword in the military milieu. In the battlefield environment, where multiple assets have to be carefully coordinated, achieving the right level of situational awareness is the key to success. Achieving real time data on common operational picture can give the combat commander a crucial advantage. The drive for unambiguous situational awareness is at the heart of the network-enabled system. This ensures enhanced collaboration and speed of command, which ultimately results in dramatically increased mission effectiveness.

The air force is in the process of creating such a system indigenously with minimal technological assistance from outside agencies. The air force has made significant progress in this very important area. The credit goes to civil IT sector for much of the innovation, with operational specifications, architecture and coding by the air force. Software technology industry is one of our pillars of strength. The software industry has a crucial role to play in the design of the avionics equipment, as nearly 30–40 per cent of systems in modern airborne platforms are software based. There is the need to strengthen our future defence programmes.

Summary of Technology Areas

Indian companies in defence business with robust technology base and skilled work force would have many opportunities in the following areas:

- Secure communication technologies
- Data and information systems
- Sensor technologies
- Guidance and control
- Electronic combat technologies
- Integrated survivability
- Technologies for remote and autonomous operation
- Power source and supply technologies
- Human performance and innovation

Defence Industrial Strategy

A well-structured aeronautics strategy covering important goals and guidelines will pave the way for a systematic development of the aeronautics industry. India's defence industry is today on the verge of transformation. The following points are very relevant.

Elements of Aeronautics Strategy

- Setting up of advanced engineering infrastructure
- Assurance of private sector participation
- Network aeronautics Industry with global aerospace community through collaboration, JVs and partnerships

- Organize key technology transfer as part of offset business strategy
- Concerted marketing drive to increase exports
- Work towards global business targets

Complex Issues

- Major Platforms – Cost Prohibitive
- Capable of continuous upgrade
- Flexibility to cater for unpredictable operational demands

Key Action Points

In order to address these issues, the Indian aeronautics industry will need to have a leading edge understanding in the following areas:

- Overall equipment design and integration
- Design and performance of subsystems
- Properties and limitations of key components
- Manage equipment modification and integration
- Through-life capability management
- Network-centric architecture
- Delivering cost effective military solutions
- To develop technical work force with innovative abilities.

Conclusion

Indian Air Force exercises diverse elements of air power to defend the Indian air space and forms an essential constituent of national security apparatus. Air power should exploit the entire spectrum of the leading-edge technology and advanced weapon systems to fulfil the roles and missions assigned to it. It is essential that in the long term our aeronautics industry must gear up to design, develop and deliver the platforms and systems specified by the air force.

To achieve this ambitious mission the following key measures need consideration:

- The government's affirmation of aeronautics industry as a key national strategic asset
- Lay down long term roadmap
- Substantially increase investment in aeronautical research and technology
- Formulate a set of durable policies for public-private partnership
- Introduce transparent planning process with close participation of the private industry.
- Promote foreign technology collaboration and investments by framing appropriate policies
- Formulate plan to generate a technically skilled workforce to run the aeronautics industry.

Our vision for the next 20 years must foresee a vibrant, technologically sophisticated and globally competitive aeronautics industry. Our new generation professional defence leadership and talented captains of the industry have the capability and confidence to build an excellent aeronautics industry. That to achieve this formidable task the government will have to provide consistent budgetary support, focused direction and proactive leadership.

Chapter 14

National Security and Higher Defence Management in India

NS Sisodia,
*IAS**

The President of India is the Supreme Commander of the Armed Forces. However, under India's parliamentary system of governance, the Cabinet Committee on Security (CCS) is the apex body responsible for all matters pertaining to national defence and security. The Cabinet Committee on Security is presided over by prime minister and its other members are: the defence minister, home minister, finance minister and minister for external affairs.

The National Security Council (NSC) which was set up in 1999, operates as a parallel body to the CCS. However, its role is advisory and all decision-making vests in the CCS. In addition to the ministers, CCS National Security Adviser is also a member

*The writer retired as Secretary, Ministry of Finance, Government of India. Presently he is Director General of IDSA and also a member of the National Security Advisory Board.

of the Council. The other supporting structures of the NSC are the National Security Advisory Board (NSAB) comprising mainly of non-official experts and a strategic policy group (SPG) headed by the cabinet secretary which includes service chiefs, secretaries of the core ministries, heads of intelligence agencies and Governor of the Reserve Bank of India. The mandate of NSAB is to provide their assessments, policy advice and other inputs to the National Security Advisor and the National Security Council. The SPG is essentially an interministerial coordination mechanism of concerned officials.

The major task of the ministry of defence is to formulate policy for India's defence and support the defence forces. The defence ministry is trichotomised into three departments, namely, department of defence, defence production, defence research and development and Ex-Servicemen welfare. A secretary heads each department. Apart from this, defence (finance) division deals with all matters having financial implications, to perform an advisory role in financial matters of the ministry.

The defence secretary heads the department of defence and coordinates activities of all other departments in the ministry. He deals with the three services, various interservice organizations and the integrated defence staff. The department of defence has the overall responsibility for defence policy, defence budget, matters relating to Parliament, defence cooperation with foreign countries and overall coordination of all defence related activities.

The chiefs of staff committee (COSC) is the apex policy mechanism of the three defence services. The three service chiefs constitute the committee, and the chief of integrated defence staff oversees the functioning of this committee. The senior most chief chairs the COSC. This committee discusses all matters, which require attention at the highest levels in the military. The COSC is the highest authority on military matters of the country. A number of sub-committees also assist the chiefs of staff committee.

Soon after India attained Independence, a number of changes came into force in India's defence set-up. The earlier set-up with a military member in the Viceroy's Council and a commander-in-chief was suited to running a colony under the British Empire. However, the principle of civilian supremacy over the military was predominant, as all matters of policy were under the domain of the secretary of war or the secretary of state for India in London. After the transfer of power, the sovereign Government of India gave this responsibility to the country's defence minister. With the creation of three chiefs of staff of equal rank and the chairman, chiefs of staff committee, the office of the commander-in-chief ended, as it no longer remained relevant under the new political dispensation.

Post-Kargil Reforms

Following the Kargil war with Pakistan and in pursuance of the recommendations of the Group of Ministers (GOM) on national security, ministry of defence created a few new structures. The GOM recognized the need for greater integration among the three services as well as between the services and ministry of defence. It, therefore, recommended creation of a post of chief of defence staff (CDS) for promoting coordination and integration of services headquarters with the ministry. The creation of the position of the CDS entails the consensus of all the political parties; however, the political parties have failed so far to arrive at any such consensus. Nevertheless, it appears that due to differences among the Services there is not much of keenness for this proposed reform. A post of chief of integrated defence staff (IDS) has however been created. The integrated defence staff is an interservice organization, which attempts to establish joint participation through integrated planning, formulation of joint concepts and doctrines, joint training, integrated operational planning and coordination in acquisition. The IDS services, both the COSC as well as the defence secretary. Recognizing the need to bring about speed and efficiency in acquisition MOD has created, a Defence Acquisition Organization whose head will be a director general. This organisation comprises officers from the three defence services, defence, finance and the department of defence.

The Emerging Challenges

With the setting up of the National Security Council apparatus and the reforms introduced in MOD following the GOM report, MOD has taken a number of useful measures to strengthen the country's defence and national security apparatus; however; these remain insufficient for meeting effectively the complex security challenges of future. The security scenario changes by the day and nobody can say when and what will happen in the future. The nature of war itself is changing. It appears that in the near future, conventional interstate wars are unlikely, even though their possibility is difficult to rule out completely, especially in India's context. With its unsettled borders and disputes with its two neighbours, defence planners have to keep in view the worst-case scenario. With two of these neighbours having nuclear weapons and the instability prevailing in India's North Western region, the security situation has become extremely fragile and complex. Although India cannot rule out a conventional conflict, asymmetric warfare has become the preferred option of weaker powers. The rise of non-state actors driven by irrational ideological and religious beliefs has brought violence to ordinary citizens' doorsteps. Thus, an environment of chronic insecurity and vulnerability prevails.

Effects of Climate Change

While our defence services have to remain prepared to face the entire spectrum of security challenges from sub-conventional warfare at one end of the spectrum to nuclear weapons exchange at the other, newer threats are emerging. Climate change leading to extreme weather events and potential disasters, acute energy shortages, water scarcity etc could further stress the security environment and precipitate intrastate or even interstate conflicts. South Asian region would be among the most vulnerable regions of the world, which is likely to suffer adverse impacts of climate change. Relatively easier availability of technical knowledge and materials can enable terrorist groups to use radiological, biological or chemical agents to create havoc among civilian communities. Pandemics and catastrophic climate changes can lead to large-scale disasters, which are difficult to deal with without the intervention of security forces.

Growth of Technology

The rapid growth of technology and accessibility of knowledge through internet and other modes of communication has further complicated the situation. Reasonably well trained terrorists can deploy sufficiently lethal and innovative devices capable of wreaking enormous damage. Developments in cyber space, nanotechnology, robotics, space technologies and genetic engineering are likely to offer potent weapons in the hands of both state and non-state actors. The modern day defence forces have to be ready to meet all possible and unpredictable challenges. To borrow from the language of a former US defence secretary, defence forces of tomorrow have to be ready for 'known knowns, known unknowns and also unknown unknowns.'

It is imperative that the structure of the future defence forces is different to take head on the unpredictable challenges effectively. The structures relevant for the large-scale tank and artillery warfare, which played an important role in earlier wars, may no longer be suitable for facing the emerging challenges. To meet a wide range of threats, flexible and smaller forces, highly trained for a variety of tasks and well equipped with state-of-the-art technologies would be more relevant. Such forces are rapidly deployable. They will have to perform tasks, which go well beyond classical war fighting. Knowledge, technology, information sharing on real time basis, sophisticated intelligence and speedy decision-making will be the secret to success in the future.

Perhaps no defence apparatus in the world is fully equipped to meet the unpredictable challenges of the future, effectively. In many countries, they are implementing radical reforms in a time bound manner to prepare for the complex threats of the future.

Preparing for the Future

The higher defence set up in India has served us well so far and our defence services have achieved some remarkable successes in the past. However, there are concerns that the reforms brought about lately may not be sufficient. What are the core areas requiring the government's attention? Some reforms, which need immediate implementation, are as follows:

The present defence planning apparatus needs more power. The country does not have a national security strategy (NSS) even after six decades of attaining freedom, despite several shocks received during the period. A national security strategy will be helpful in providing policy guidelines not only to defence services but also other concerned agencies and ministries, like the ministry of external affairs, home affairs, civil aviation and transport and shipping.

National Security Strategy

A National Security strategy links ends and means, offers a coherent plan of action and facilitates coordinated action among all concerned security agencies, even those outside the government. A national security strategy formulated through a consultative process prepares the groundwork for synergistic action. The National Security Council with its support structures, which can ensure coordinated assessments and planning through the National Security Adviser, can best accomplish this task. The exercise can then provide a solid basis for long term and realistic defence planning, synthesizing inputs of all the concerned official and non-official agencies.

The higher echelons of ministry of defence also need freedom from some of the operational pressures so that they can devote greater attention to long-term planning and policy formulation. A culture of chronic fire fighting which often prevails can hardly be conducive to planning and policy work. It is equally vital that systems and structures need reform in the higher defence set-up to make sound and integrated defence planning possible. Currently, despite some recent improvements, defence plans remain undeveloped in the context of a coherent national security strategy. Essentially, they are aggregations of plans of individual defence services. They focus on acquisition of equipment rather than on development of long-term capabilities. Interservices prioritization based on cost benefit analysis of available options is not undertaken. Each service tends to enlarge its role and holdings with no integrated approach to maximize overall defence effectiveness. It was in this background that the Group of Ministers had recommended creation of the post of chief of defence staff (CDS). In his absence, the task of interservice prioritisation falls on officials of ministry of defence or ministry of finance. It is a task, which they are not equipped to perform for lack of in-depth knowledge or authority. In case, creation of a chief of defence staff is inappropriate in the Indian context, there is urgent need to explore the alternatives for bringing about coordination and cooperation of joint and several levels among the three arms of the military. The present set-up of chairman, chiefs of staff committee should have undiluted authority so that it can become an effective coordinating mechanism or else the government should create the post of Joint Chiefs of Staff.

Their mandates, however, should suit the Indian context. Some experts feel that such reform is possible only through legislation as was the case of the United States. The ministry of defence itself needs a mindset change. There is need to adopt several feasible measures. Firstly, civilians and military officials in the ministry of defence should serve for sufficiently long tenures. It is usual in the UK, for instance, for permanent under secretaries to serve for more than five years. In India, defence secretaries have brief tenures. This principle is equally applicable for other senior officers both in the armed forces and in the ministry who are engaged in the policy and planning work. Secondly, the expertise of the armed forces need full utilization by greater integration of defence officers in the ministry. Both civilians and the armed forces need to be part of a common team as they serve a common cause. Thirdly, the ministry of defence is in need of more attention for capacity building of ministry officials and for induction of highly qualified experts and analysts in the relevant disciplines. They should be able to offer their independent analysis to the minister without any service or institutional biases. The decision-making processes in the ministry of defence, particularly in the area of acquisition are notoriously cumbersome and slow. These need a drastic reform through simplification of procedures, delegation and decentralization of authority, use of information technology to the extent possible and creation of databases. Greater specialization, capacity building and domain expertise would also help in informed and speedier decision-making. Capacity building of civilians in the domain of defence, who are otherwise competent, is vital, as with limited knowledge in matters of defence, many of them may not be equipped to participate constructively in decision-making process. They should be able to add value to proposals received from the Services' Headquarters. It is not their capacity or commitment, but the present system of generalist culture, which handicaps them. This problem is redressable.

Another core area requiring attention is the development of a truly integrated and multi-disciplinary Defence Acquisition

Organization. The task of acquiring modern day defence weapons and equipment, which employ cutting-edge technologies is complex. It calls for technical knowledge, operational experience, expertise in law and contracting, financial analysis and negotiating skills, among others. Industrialized countries like the US, the UK and France, have highly integrated and specialized acquisition organizations. They are able to procure for their defence forces the best possible equipment, at affordable costs and in a timely manner. India's record of accomplishment of acquiring defence equipment has been encouraging—ignoring the inordinate delays that occurred in the past. The government can solve this problem by strengthening the present defence acquisition organization.

Finally, a sense of greater participation of defence forces at higher level decision-making is the immediate need of the day and is possible through reforms. Future contingencies may not afford much time for consultations amongst political leaders, civilians and top levels of the armed forces. These have to take place in advance for contingencies both known and unknown, with active participation of military leaders.

So far, attention has been given mainly to addressing the country's external threats, but as external and internal security challenges are blurred and as the distinction between combatants and civilians are dissolved, greater attention needs to be given, integrating external and internal security strategies.

The higher National Security and Defence Management set-up has served us reasonably satisfactorily, so far. The government has made serious efforts to reform the structures, by learning lessons from the past. However, given the complex security scenario we are bound to face in the future, there is need for continuing review of and reforms in the higher national security and defence management structures.

Index

Notes

Notes

Notes

Notes